Fifty Years in Phonetics

Selected Papers

Fifty Years in Phonetics

Selected Papers

David Abercrombie

Language most shows a man:
speak, that I may see thee.

Ben Jonson

Talk is a deplorably polluting fate that could
happen to the best sentence.

Dr Jonathan Miller

EDINBURGH UNIVERSITY PRESS

© David Abercrombie 1991

Edinburgh University Press
22 George Square, Edinburgh

Set in Linotronic Times Roman by
Koinonia Limited, Bury, and
printed in Great Britain by
Redwood Press Limited, Melksham, Wiltshire

Distributed in the United States of America by
Columbia University Press, New York

British Library Cataloguing
   in Publication Data
Abercrombie, David
   Fifty years in phonetics.
1. Phonetics
I. Title
414

ISBN 0 7486 0196 1

Contents

To
Alexandra Gaylord
in gratitude for her invaluable
advice and help

Foreword

Ten years have elapsed since the Memoir, which opens this collection of papers, was privately circulated, and also since I retired from my post at Edinburgh University. I did not retire from academic life, however. I had the good fortune almost immediately to be offered an appointment, for a year, in the Department of Linguistics, of which J. M. Y. Simpson was head, at the University of Glasgow. It is sad that such an excellent department should now have closed down. This, and other things, make the optimism expressed in the final paragraph of Chapter 1 about the future of the subject seem perhaps premature.

I was fortunate once again in being able to have the index to this collection of papers prepared by L. A. Iles, who has also given me much valuable advice. I have already expressed, in the dedication, my indebtedness to Alexandra Gaylord. My wife Mary helped at all stages in the preparation of the manuscript. I am most grateful to them and to the many others whose comments and criticisms have contributed to this somewhat miscellaneous collection of papers.

1

Fifty Years: A Memoir

Published in *Work in Progress* No. 13, 1980. Reprinted in *Forum Linguisticum*
Vol. 5 No. 2, 1980

I went to University College London as a postgraduate student in the
Phonetics Department, following the advice of Daniel Jones, in the
autumn of 1930. I was on the books of the college as a postgraduate
student for seven years, though I was doing various other things too at
the same time. I think I learnt a lot of phonetics in those seven years.

The University College Phonetics Department at that time was
divided, geographically and ideologically, into two parts: upstairs and
downstairs. Upstairs was presided over by Daniel Jones; downstairs by
Stephen Jones (no relation). I can make this dichotomy clearer by
explaining how the premises of the Department were laid out.

It was housed in – it occupied the whole of – what was known as Arts
Annexe No. 1. This in fact was, or had been, one of the houses of Gordon
Square, but you entered it from the College, through the back door and not
through the front door from Gordon Square (though nowadays people use
the front door – the Department has not moved). You entered at the
ground-floor level, where the Department office was, presided over by the
formidable Miss Parkinson, or Parky, as she was known to everyone,
Daniel Jones's secretary. From there you could go down by a dark
staircase to what had been the kitchens of the original house, but which
now constituted the Phonetics Laboratory, of which Stephen Jones was
Superintendent. Or, you could go up by another staircase to the lecture
rooms and the rooms of the rest of the staff, with Mlle Coustenoble and
Miss Ida Ward right up at the top. Daniel Jones's room was on the first
floor. J. R. Firth and Miss Sophie 'Lund ("marraine" as she was called) had
rooms on the ground floor. So, when one entered the Department, one
could go *upstairs* to Daniel Jones and most of his colleagues, or *downstairs*
to Stephen Jones and his laboratory and a different world.

I lived happily in both worlds while I was in the Department, and I derived enormous benefit from both of them. Let me start by saying something of the downstairs world.

The laboratory in the basement still had the original kitchen range in it, with a fire burning most of the year with a kettle on it and a teapot on the hob, which made it a very pleasant and sociable place to be, especially on a raw November evening. Firth spent a great deal of his time there: though geographically he belonged to upstairs, spiritually he belonged to downstairs.

I too spent a lot of time there. I took Stephen Jones's course in Experimental Phonetics, in which a lot of the tuition was individual, and I enjoyed it greatly. Stephen Jones – Steve, as he was always known – was a nice, kind, generous man, and a fine teacher. But in addition I spent many hours gossiping with Steve and Firth, and other occasional visitors, about the present state and current problems of Phonetics. The gossip was most educative.

Firth and Steve were very critical of much of what went on in the rest of the Department, of what they called upstairs Phonetics. They did not doubt their colleagues' practical abilities as phoneticians, but they did not like the way the Department was organised around teaching the pronunciation of foreign languages, even though this was done with remarkable efficiency. The phonetics upstairs was nearly all applied phonetics (to use an expression which long antedated the expression "applied linguistics"). They objected also to the lack of interest in theory, to the fact that students were never recommended to read books, and to the disregard of what was being said elsewhere by other people. They objected to the very segmental approach of the upstairs phoneticians, and their neglect of, and lack of interest in, the syllable. I had not been long in the Department before Steve lent me, and strongly advised me to read, Stetson's *Motor Phonetics*, which had come out a couple of years earlier. I could not get people upstairs to discuss it.

Steve and Firth thought little of the upstairs phoneme theory, which was, of course, Daniel Jones's phoneme theory. In particular, it seemed to them to be of no help with a problem much discussed at that time: what size of unit best explains the way speech is innervated by the speaker and perceived by the hearer. Incidentally, a motor theory of perception was the one most favoured downstairs. 'It is possible to exaggerate the importance of the ear in speech', Stephen Jones wrote.

Another topic which aroused considerable interest downstairs but not much upstairs was rhythm, though a great deal of work was done upstairs on intonation.

Judgements on people that were made upstairs were thought downstairs to be curiously limited. Firth was most amused when he said to Daniel Jones, after I had been working in the Department a while, 'What do you think of Abercrombie?' and Jones answered only, 'Well, his Cardinal Three's not very good.

I was particularly attracted by the downstairs outlook on phonetic matters because when I first went there I was working on my M.A. thesis for the Universityof Leeds, the title of which was 'The Phonetic Basis of i-Mutation'; I felt that the traditional, segment-based explanation of how i-mutation came about was unconvincing, and I was looking for an explanation more on the lines of vowel harmony.

Downstairs was exciting and stimulating. So, to me, was upstairs. Daniel Jones's colleagues were marvellous phoneticians, and I was taught by nearly all of them. I valued greatly the sensory training they gave me.

Almost no general phonetic theory was taught in the Department, at least not formally. There were no classes in general phonetic performance, except for the Cardinal Vowels (which I was taught by Daniel Jones). Apart from this, all performance training was in a language. I was taught to perform, that is to say to read aloud from phonetic texts, in French (above all – three or four hours a week), German, Danish, Urdu, Sechuana, Sinhalese, Cantonese, and other languages that I have forgotten about. Almost all the teaching was tête-à-tête, and it was very intensive and rigorous – perfection was demanded. It was exhausting.

I took a lot of classes with Daniel Jones, and he taught me alone in nearly all of them. He sometimes taught lying down; he had a large leather-covered couch in his room for that purpose. It was always said that he was a chronic invalid; at any rate, he was shielded from the world, and from all exertion and worry, by a devoted band of ladies, his secretary and his lecturers.As a result of their ministrations, he died at the age of 86.

Learning the Cardinal Vowels from Jones was a long and painful process, and it did not include learning how to use them in phonetic description of languages. That was left to Ida Ward (later to be Professor of African Languages), and very well she did it.

The Phonetics Department taught other subjects besides phonetics: speech therapy, for example (Ida Ward had written a book on the subject); but more importantly General Linguistics, in which courses were given by Firth, and Applied Linguistics (as it would now be called), i.e. methods of teaching English to foreign learners, in which courses were given by Hyacinth Davies. Both of these were well done, and I profited greatly from them.

There were two Phonetics Departments in London University at that time; the other one was at the School of Oriental Studies. Professor Arthur Lloyd James was its head. It was a small department; the other member of staff was Raymond Butlin. The former was ideologically an upstairs man, and the latter a downstairs one. Lloyd James was at that time a well-known and influential figure because of his frequent broadcasts and articles in newspapers, and because he was Adviser on Spoken English to the BBC. R. T. Butlin was Senior Lecturer. He had been one of the most brilliant students of the U.C. Department. I became a frequent visitor to the School.

As far as I know, there were no other Phonetics Departments in Britain.

Daniel Jones and Lloyd James were very good at looking after the welfare of young phoneticians, and were able to get them a variety of jobs. This was partly because most of us were in need of money (there were no grants in those days!), and partly because it was considered that part of the education of young phoneticians lay in teaching or lecturing. It seems remarkable looking back, how much at that time phoneticians were in demand for various purposes. I became involved almost immediately with two projects which greatly enlarged my experience, and which are worth mentioning briefly.

The first was with Robert Bridges, who was then Poet Laureate. Bridges was publishing his collected essays, and he wanted them to be in a reformed spelling which he had devised, which had a large number of new letters. He felt he needed advice on phonetic matters (Bernard Shaw, in the preface to *Pygmalion*, calls Bridges a phonetician, but he was not). I had a number of talks with him at his house in Oxford, and later, after he died, with his wife, who took over the project. The essays came out, published by Oxford University Press, in seven beautifully printed volumes. He had the help of the great typographer Stanley Morison in designing the new letters.

The other was with a lady scholar, Miss Melian Stawell. She was greatly interested in Cretan scripts, and was convinced that the language they represented was Greek, which was not at that time a popular view. Although she was an extremely learned lady, she believed she needed the help of a phonetician with her decipherment. Her book on the subject came out in 1931, and most people did not find it convincing; however, Michael Ventris has since shown that at least one of the scripts, Linear B, very probably was Greek.

Working with Robert Bridges and Mrs Bridges, and with Melian Stawell, gave me an interest in writing systems very early on which I have never lost. It was an interest of which Firth strongly approved, and one which was reinforced when, a few years later, I came to work on the history of shorthand and especially on the achievements of Isaac Pitman.

These most interesting projects were not financially rewarded, however; but thanks to Daniel Jones and Arthur Lloyd James I became involved in a number of other things which were, and which were also very instructive. They concerned mostly teaching English pronunciation, and sometimes teaching English as a whole, to foreigners; but also other applications of the subject. For example, it was widely and firmly believed during the first half of this century that the only efficient way to teach a language was through its spoken form. Probably more balanced views prevail now; but in those days it was held to be true not only of modern languages but of the classical languages as well. Both Latin and Greek were taught at many schools by the Direct Method, with no use of English and no reference in the early stages to written forms. Daniel Jones got me a job lecturing on teaching the pronunciation of Latin to the annual summer school of the Association for the Reform of Latin Teaching. I did not have to lecture in Latin, fortunately. It was a help that I myself had learnt Latin and Greek at school in this way. I lectured at the summer school for several years.

I had only been in the Department a few months when I was invited to take part in the Quinzaine Anglaise of the Association France-Grande Bretagne, thanks to Daniel Jones and Lloyd James. It was held in the Sorbonne, in July, and the first week of the Quinzaine was devoted to pronunciation and spoken English. Lloyd James himself, assisted by Raymond Butlin, usually did the teaching, but that year Lloyd James was unable to take part, and so Raymond Butlin took his place, assisted by me. Fifty school teachers attended, and it was a daunting experience. I was just twenty-one; it was like being thrown in at the deep end.

Another valuable experience was teaching English to the members of the Soviet trade delegation, Arcos (made famous by the 'Arcos raid'). It was a big delegation, and a number of other young phoneticians took part in the teaching.

Postgraduate phonetics students gave a great deal of private tuition. One of the most interesting private pupils who came my way was the Japanese Ambassador, a most intelligent and charming man, but badly in need of tuition. He later became Prime Minister of Japan – Shigeru Yoshida. I well remember an occasion when I got an early morning call asking me to go urgently to the Japanese Embassy. It turned out that our ambassador in China had been machine-gunned, while riding in his car which had a Union Jack painted on the roof, by a Japanese fighter plane. Anthony Eden had summoned Yoshida at once to the Foreign Office for an explanation. Unfortunately Yoshida was quite unable to pronounce our wounded ambassador's name, which was Knatchbull-Hugesson – a name which raises a number of problems for a Japanese, and Yoshida needed emergency tuition in it.

The large number of other private pupils who came to me contributed greatly to my phonetic education; I learnt a lot, not only about how to teach pronunciation, but about my pupils' various mother tongues.

It was considered in those days that a phonetician ought to be able to *speak* a language other than his own, as well as being able to pronounce it. Henry Sweet was of the same opinion, and he thought that the ideal language for an English-speaking phonetician to learn was French, since the two languages differed from each other in so many respects. The University College Phonetics Department also thought the language should be French.

I did not know any French, beyond what I had done at school up to the matriculation level. So when Daniel Jones one day asked me 'How's your spoken French?', I had to answer that it was non-existent. Jones said that they could not have that; and he therefore arranged for me to go to Paris as Assistant Anglais at the Lycée Louis-le-Grand. I was there for two years. I lived in the Lycée, and I learnt French. I started by going systematically through the book, by Daniel Jones and H.M. Stéphan, which accompanied the HMV recorded course in French, a book which I have always considered to be much the best introductory course to a language ever written.

I was in Paris from 1931 to 1933. I visited the Department at University College whenever I was home on vacation, but I also became a student at the Institut de Phonétique, of which Pierre Fouché was Director. I enjoyed being there, but I missed both the enthusiasm and the rigorous teaching that one found at University College. The most valuable course I took there was, curiously enough, one on how to read French verse aloud.

The most memorable event of my time in France was when I took the IPA Certificate. Nowadays people take the examination in English, but in those days, if English was your mother tongue, it was understood that you took the examination in French. The IPA examiner in France was Paul Passy, and one had to go to his farm, which was a large socialist commune, to take the examination.

One went there by train from Paris, with two changes, and stayed the night at a little hotel in a village, from where one walked next morning to the farm – it was quite a long walk, almost an hour. The hotel was quite accustomed to having candidates for the examination staying there, and was able to give clear directions on how to get to the farm. The examination, which started about 9 a.m., was long and exacting, and Passy's great-granddaughter was born in the room next door in the middle of it. I passed the examination – Passy said I did very well – and was asked to stay to lunch, with all the other members (there were about twenty of them) of the commune. Passy, dressed in peasant clothes, and over six foot tall, was enormously impressive, both as a man and as a phonetician. I consider myself most fortunate to have met him.

There were very few academic posts in phonetics in those days, and when I came back from my two years in Paris there did not seem much chance of my getting one. Instead, I got a job at the London School of Economics, in the Modern Languages Department, thanks, once again, to Lloyd James. The job was teaching English to foreign students for the B.Com. and B.Sc.(Econ.) degrees, and also taking some part in the teaching of French. I was in sole charge of the teaching of English, and was probably the only person teaching English as a foreign language as a degree subject in a British university.

I had a colleague at LSE who was at that time very influential in linguistics – the anthropologist Bronislaw Malinowski. I had already attended the seminar on linguistics which he gave at the School of Oriental Studies, the seminar which resulted in the second volume of his book *Coral Gardens*. Firth, Lloyd James, Butlin, and other phoneticians also attended it. I got to know Malinowski quite well, and conversations with him over morning coffee or afternoon tea were another important part of my education. LSE was the best-run institution I ever taught in, and I was very happy there.

Another person who influenced me greatly about this time was C.K. Ogden, the inventor of Basic English, translator of Wittgenstein, co-author of *The Meaning of Meaning*, and author or translator of numerous other books, who appeared to spend all his time in conversation, and

was never observed to do any work. He seemed to be very rich; he had
two houses in Bloomsbury, one in Cambridge, one in the Peak district,
and a flat in Brighton. He lived in all of them, and I remember being
impressed by the fact that he had a copy of the poems of Gerard Manley
Hopkins in every room of every house, so that he could always refer to
them instantly if he needed to. He did not believe in being put to any
trouble. He had a superb library of books on linguistics, which he left
to University College. He was a polymath, and once wrote a review of
the *Encyclopaedia Britannica*. I have never met a more entertaining
talker, though he was also an exhausting one. I devised the phonetic
transcription that he used in the *General Basic Dictionary* (which is still
in print).

Ogden was an amateur in linguistics in the sense that he made no
money out of it, and never had a job in it (or in anything else). Another
amateur at that time was Sir Richard Paget, who wrote a number of
books on language, the best known of which was *Human Speech*. He
was a man of remarkable talents. One of his accomplishments was the
ability to turn his hands into an artificial talking device, with a bellows-
operated reed between his two thumbs. He used to demonstrate it in
public, and he claimed it was particularly useful when one was in the
dentist's chair, because he could make his hands say 'Look out! You're
on the nerve.' He devised a sign language for the deaf, and made a film
of it; it is now, I believe, sponsored by the RNID. He and his daughter,
each whistling and humming simultaneously, could perform string
quartets together, a most remarkable feat. I met him several times.

A notable event which took place while I was at University College
was the Second International Congress of Phonetic Sciences. It lasted
a week; it was nice and small – about 250 people; all the papers were
brief and were not pre-circulated. It was attended by many famous
figures: Jespersen, Vendryès, Trubetzkoy, Jakobson, Stetson, Scripture,
to name but a few.

The phoneme was the main preoccupation of the Congress, both in
the papers and in informal discussion. Of particular interest were were
two papers from the Danish glossematicians (who were not yet called
that) Hjelmslev and Uldall, delivered in their immaculate English. It
was from these papers, I am quite sure, that Firth got the term *prosody*,
used as a countable noun, as a name for a phonological unit. Firth never
acknowledged this, and as far as I know attention has never been drawn
to it. Firth certainly listened to both papers. Hjelmslev's was entitled
'On the principles of Phonematics', and Uldall's was 'The Phonematics

of Danish'. Both are still worth reading.

Upstairs phonetics finally prevailed at University College. Stephen Jones retired, and Dennis Fry became Superintendant of the laboratory. Firth went to the School of Oriental Studies, or SOAS as it became. He took the downstairs outlook with him, and prosodic theory was born there; but its gestation was downstairs at University College.

All the time that I was engaged in other things, I was determined eventually to get an academic job in Phonetics. There were a number of things I wanted to do in the subject, or perhaps I should say with the subject.

Phonetics, in its early days, tended, as an academic subject, to be a bit odd. I think it suffered from the fact that phoneticians were often mixed up with various 'movements', some worthy, some cranky, but all involving fervent propaganda. I have in mind such things as the reform of methods of language teaching, the advocacy of shorthand for the masses, the reform of English orthography. A regular speaker on Sundays at Marble Arch in those days used to carry a banner with the words 'Henry Sweet' written on it.

Another eccentricity was that articles in the subject's chief journal were printed in phonetic transcription, so that most people could not read them, and even those who could usually did not want to.

I felt I would like to do something to make phonetics less associated in people's minds with crankiness.

Another problem was that general phonetics was not considered to be a possible undergraduate subject (neither was linguistics). The greater part of academic phoneticians' time in those days was occupied with pronunciation teaching; the subject was almost entirely an ancillary one. A Phonetics Department, for the most part, was a service department to the Modern Language Departments. 'Pure', as opposed to 'applied', phonetics was only taught at the postgraduate level, and then hardly ever in formally organised courses.

I had ambitions to try to make phonetics not only a *normal* subject, but also an undergraduate subject comparable in status to other undergraduate subjects. I spent a great deal of my spare time during the Second World War working out what an undergraduate course in phonetics would consist of.

When the War was over I went back to my old job at LSE, but when the University of Leeds advertised a lectureship in Phonetics in the English Language Department I applied for it and got it. I was able to get an undergraduate course in General Phonetics adopted in the

Faculty of Arts. It was a one-year course, with the possibility of it becoming, later, a two-year or even a three-year course. However, I was able to teach only the first year of the course, because I was invited by Edinburgh University to start a Phonetics Department there in the autumn of 1948. I was able to get an Ordinary Course in Phonetics established, modelled on the Leeds course, but with five hours a week instead of three. Like many other Ordinary Courses, it was attended by a wide variety of students, including honours students and postgraduates, and some students from other faculties, and, for the first few years, a number of members of staff. The course was a great pleasure to teach. It was first given in the session 1949-50. Many academic phoneticians in the world today were recruited from it.

Phonetics has been accepted as an undergraduate subject since then and, some years later, so has Linguistics.

I do not really see many changes in the subject since I entered it over fifty years ago. Of course, technological advances, and especially electronic ones, have made the laboratory a very different place, and the advent of the tape recorder was a great boon to phoneticians, indeed to all students of language. Magnetic recording systems had, of course, been in existence for a long time – since the beginning of the century; but they were either of poor quality or beyond the reach of Phonetics Departments. Systems such as the Blattnerphone or Marconi-Stille were far too expensive, and the recordings, which were made on steel ribbon, were bulky and heavy and were not intended for storage. Only broadcasting stations used such systems. Other people, such as Phonetics Departments or dialect fieldworkers, had to use disc recording. There were wire recorders, it is true, but the recordings they made were of very poor quality.

So the discovery that you could use, instead of steel ribbon, paper or plastic tape surfaced or impregnated with a ferrous compound was a revolutionary one for the subject. The German Magnetophone came first, as I remember, followed by the American Soundmirror, and of course now there are innumerable cheap and convenient tape-recording devices.

The sound spectrograph, fibre-optics, and synthetic speech devices are all advances which have made a great difference to teaching and research in phonetics.

Synthetic speech, incidentally, has quite a long history in Edinburgh University, starting with the collaboration of Fleeming Jenkin and J.A. Ewing, who synthesised a number of vowels as long ago as 1870.

Fleeming Jenkin was Professor of Engineering; his biography was written by Robert Louis Stevenson. J.A. Ewing was to become Principal of the University. They published many papers together, particularly on the analysis and synthesis of vowels.

The establishment of phonetics as a bona fide academic subject, and the benefits to instrumental and experimental phonetics of technological advances, are perhaps the most noticeable changes that I have seen. Of course, many more languages have been described phonetically and phonologically since I started in the field, and our knowledge of the phonetic capabilities of man has consequently grown greatly. But questions such as whether the phoneme has any role in the perception of speech, or in the programming of his utterances by the speaker, are still as much a matter for argument as they were fifty years ago. New phonological theories are still appearing, as they were then, often claiming, as they did then, to be 'the only genuine theory of phonology in existence' (I quote from what James Foley says of his own theory in his book *Foundations of Theoretical Phonology*).

But I look back nostalgically on those early, more spacious and leisurely days, with the academic world, and particularly the linguistic world, so much smaller than it is now. There was not the pressure to publish that there is now, or to take higher degrees. People seemed to be less touchy; controversy was less disagreeable than it is now.

I do not think I would prophesy with confidence about the future of the subject, though I think various things are threatening it at the moment. Nevertheless, I remain optimistic. I heard R.W. Langacker give a very remarkable paper at a conference a few years ago. In it he said that there are two kinds of animals in Linguistics: unicorns and coyotes. Unicorns are noble animals concerned with noble things like the construction of all-embracing theories. Coyotes, on the other hand, spend their time grubbing about in the mess of linguistic facts. It seems to me that phoneticians are among the coyotes – indeed Langacker said so. And the last words of his paper were 'the coyotes will inherit the earth'. I hope he is right; I believe he is.

2

Phonetics and Phonology

Paper given, on 13 March 1978, to the Third Inter-Collegiate Linguistics
Conference, University of Wales, held at Gregynog. Circulated privately in
Work in Progress No 12, 1979.

For quite a long time the two words *phonetics* and *phonology* existed
side by side, meaning more or less the same thing. *Phonology* is about
half a century older; but after the word *phonetics* came into language,
the two tended to be used indifferently. They both meant simply 'the
study of speech sounds'. (One of the meanings given by the OED for
phonology is 'phonetics', and one of the meanings given there for
phonetics is 'phonology') Although there was little sign, during most
of the time, of either word taking on a consistent specialisation of
meaning in any direction, perhaps some slight tendency could
be observed for *phonetics* to be the term used when discussing
non-language-specific, general human, matters; and for *phonology*
to be used when the sounds of a particular language were under
discussion or description. Nevertheless, the words were more or less
synonyms.

Synonyms are wasteful, especially where technical terms are concerned. S. T. Coleridge observed that in all societies there is 'a certain
collective, unconscious good sense working progressively to
desynonymize those words originally of the same meaning', [1] usually
by specialising the meaning of one member of a synonymous pair. The
emerging tendency to distinguish the uses of *phonetics* and *phonology*
was potentially fruitful; clearly the pair were ripe for desynonymisation,
and *phonology* was the term destined for specialisation. Otto Jespersen
advocated this in 1924:

> It is possible to have a theory of human speech-sounds in general
> ... By the side of this we have the theory of what is peculiar to the
> one particular language with which the grammarian is concerned
> ... It would, perhaps, be advisable to restrict the word 'phonetics'

to universal or general phonetics and to use the word 'phonology' of the phenomena peculiar to a particular language.[2]

What Jespersen thought was advisable is what happened, and it
gave rise to two specialisations in meaning of the word *phonology*, one
of which was short-lived, and the other long-lived. The 'phenomena
peculiar to a particular language' could be considered either diachron-
ically or synchronically. It was the former, the diachronic or historical,
specialisation that emerged first. It had in fact already been adopted by
Henry Sweet as early as 1908,[3] and by the time I became an undergraduate, not very long after Jespersen was writing, that was the sense
given to *phonology* in most of what I had to read. *Phonetics* continued
to be used to mean the general, non-language-specific, study.[4]

As it turned out, this specialisation, though clearly a useful one, was
not a very long-lived meaning of *phonology*, and by now it seems to be
more or less dead. (It did not emerge, incidentally, in time to get into
the OED.) What killed it was another, new, specialisation of meaning:
the use of the word for the synchronic study of the 'phenomena
peculiar to a particular language', which amounts to the study of
sounds as members of a system rather than of sounds in themselves.
The idea of a sound-system for a language, lying behind its meaning-
carrying sound-patterns, was of course not a new one. W. D. Whitney,
for example, wrote in 1875 of English as having 'an orderly system of
sounds' with 'lines and degrees of relationship which bind its members
together'.[5] But there was no special name for the study of such
synchronic systems until the Linguistic Circle of Prague put forward
the word *phonology* (and the corresponding words in other languages)
for it. The *phoneme* was, of course, the central concept in this new
sense of phonology.

I well remember, though, the strong resistance that there was at first
in many circles, both in Europe and in the USA, to this new application
of the word, which emerged while I was still a student. With the change
in emphasis in linguistic studies everywhere at that time from the
diachronic to the synchronic, however, it was bound to prevail. A
number of consequences, not all of which, probably, were foreseen,
followed from the eventual well-nigh universal acceptance of this
sense of *phonology*, which I think we may now regard as irrevocably
established. I want to look at how phonology, so understood, has come
to be related to phonetics.

General phonetics was seen as the *ally* of phonology in the earlier,
diachronic, specialisation of its sense. Sound-changes, for example

had to be explained on grounds provided by phonetics, grounds for what could be called general phonetic reasonableness. But the relation between the new sense of phonology and general phonetics was more ambiguous; phonetics was no longer clearly an ally.

There appeared, almost at once, a tendency to set up phonology as a discipline distinct and separate from phonetics, instead of regarding phonetics and phonology as two different but related ways of looking at the same phenomena. Many succumbed to the temptation to do this. Not so much in Britain, it should be said, or at least not until recently; both Daniel Jones and J. R. Firth, probably the two most influential figures in linguistics here this century, were strongly opposed to any such tendency. But two other very influential figures, one in Europe, Prince Trubetzkoy, and one in America, Leonard Bloomfield, claimed that phonology *was* a separate discipline, and thanks to their prestige many people followed them.

When phonetics and phonology are divorced from each other in this way, it somehow seems to come about that phonetics is given a more humble part to play, in one way or another. The people who practise it, 'phoneticians', who are now different people from 'phonologists', tend to be looked on as, so to speak, the hewers of wood and drawers of water – indispensable, perhaps, but essentially menial. The phonologists' is a loftier pursuit, a more intellectual one. And K. L. Pike said 'Phonetics gathers raw material. Phonemics [i.e. phonology] cooks it'. A mere gatherer of foodstuffs, one cannot help observing, has a more lowly role than the cook, and is more likely to be considered an artisan than an artist. (I do not think, though, that Pike, perhaps the most talented living phonetician, really intended to belittle his own subject by this aphorism. And the word 'cook' has a curious double meaning here, which could, when you think about it, be uncomplimentary to phonology. I will return to this ambiguity later.)

Nobody doubts, moreover, that phonology is a linguistic study, while phonetics is often said to be at best pre-linguistic. And phonology is called a *social* science, making it appear to be a more *human* subject than phonetics, which is classed as a *natural* science – one that is not concerned with people.

Phonetics came to be regarded not only as the more humble member of the pair; some people considered it to be a potential nuisance in addition. As Bloomfield put it, phoneticians 'sometimes acquire great virtuosity in discriminating and reproducing all manner of strange sounds. In this there lies some danger for linguistic work.' This unfortunate virtuosity leads phoneticians – since they cannot resist making public what they know – to 'clutter up their transcriptions' with matters that are not scientifically relevant. The implication is that although you cannot do without phoneticians, they must be kept in their place.

There is a story, as a matter of fact, that, as early as the nineteenth century, phonetics was more than a potential nuisance: it had become a real menace to the whole of linguistic study. E. H. Sturtevant's *Introduction to Linguistic Science* contains what he claims to be a description of the state of affairs at the turn of the century:

> As phonetic observation became more detailed and exact, scholars saw that they must recognise vastly more phonetic variation than they had supposed. The resulting complications made it more and more difficult to state problems in historical comparative grammar, and some were inclined to despair of finding any solutions whatever .... Some simplification was necessary if linguistic science was to continue.[6]

The fortunate discovery of the phoneme concept provided the simplification, and the phonology thus became the saviour of linguistic science. Thanks to phonology, people were able to stop despairing and get on with their work.

A curious thing about this story is that, if it is true, it provides a rare instance in science – perhaps the only instance – of a lot of knowledge being a dangerous thing, an obstacle to further advance. The achievement of phonology, it is claimed, was to counteract the unfortunate effects of knowing too much.

But an even more curious thing about the story is that it is not true. There is no evidence whatever that philologists, or other people concerned with language, ever thought themselves to be in such a predicament; and no evidence that the techniques of phonetics (which had been good for a long time) were beginning to clutter up observations with useless minutiae.

It is strange, therefore, that the story should continue to crop up, in various forms. It is mentioned, for instance, by F. W. Householder (who speaks of the 'morass of phonetic hair-splitting that the phonemic principle was intended to extricate us from long ago'); by Robert Lado (who credits Henry Sweet with both creating the problem and solving it); by E. C. Fudge ('As the discipline of phonetics developed during the second half of the nineteenth century, and the task of phonetic transcription became more and more complex ...'); by Robert A. Hall

Jr (who says 'it came to be a mark of virtuosity in a phonetician to distinguish as many different sounds as possible'; Daniel Jones, for example, 'could hear 120 different vowel sounds in English'). It was even claimed that phoneticians were not only a danger to others but they were also their own worst enemy and a danger to their own subject: 'increased accuracy of observation seemed to threaten it in its foundations' (Haas).[7] This prevalence of myth is unhealthy.

The separation of phonology from phonetics has been bad for both; after the divorce, they tend less and less to keep a needed restraining hand on each other. Phonetics, for example, should always be (to use a phrase which has recently become fashionable but which in fact has long standing in the literature) linguistic phonetics, i.e. phonetics informed by phonological knowledge, even when such things as drunken speech, pathological speech, speech acquisition by the child, are under investigation. But what phoneticians do is not always truly linguistic phonetics, particularly in some of the phonetics laboratories of Europe, where vocal noises have sometimes been studied in isola- tion from the people who produce them and the purpose for which they were produced – with consequent prejudice, often, to the value of the results of the study.

Phonology, too, has suffered: the divorce has tended to have the effect of alienating it from real spoken language, from phonetic facts. It may be a social science, but it nevertheless seems at times far removed from the study of the activities of actual people when talking or listening. It is widely believed that one can base phonological analysis on second-hand observation. The author of a work on the phonology of Japanese, for example, tells us in his Preface that his informants were 'dictionaries and textbooks rather than live persons'.

The paradoxical result of what came to be called 'rephonemi- cisation' is that much contemporary phonology is concerned not with spoken but with *written* language; it may be written in phonetic (or 'phonemic') transcription, but all the same it is *visual* symbols that are being discussed and manipulated. Notation has usurped the place of what it stands for. I agree, as I have said elsewhere, with the math- ematician Hyman Levy that 'notation is the very life-blood of science', but its connection with what it refers to ought not to be lost sight of; notation is not a substitute for reality.

Trubetzkoy said that 'the phonetic concepts with which the pho- nologist operates appear of necessity somewhat schematised and simplified' which, he added, ought not to disappoint the phonetician.

In other words, what phonologists say to phoneticians about the data the latter produce is 'we, for *our* purposes, do not need it *all*'; and this seems fair enough – provided, nevertheless, it is remembered that you cannot be sure about what you need until you *have* it all. All the same, phonology must be allowed to select, omit, and generalise. This, however, should not entail plain misrepresentation of the facts; it often seems to, though.

Thus, for example, when some phonologists say that certain vowels in Thai are *central* unrounded vowels and a protest is made that they are unmistakably *back* unrounded vowels, it is not satisfactory to reply that it makes things seem more symmetrical to call them central. Sanford Schane, on the other hand, has claimed that the category of central unrounded vowels is not needed in phonology at all because they are 'perceptually similar to back unrounded ones', with which they may be classed.[8] (They are also perceptually similar, as has often been pointed out, to front rounded ones – more so perhaps; one wonders why they should not rather be classed with the latter.) The consequence of this view is that the second vowel in English *roses* is called by Schane 'high back unrounded'.

A cavalier attitude to phonetic reality leads to the belief that awkward facts can always be adjusted or ignored: the raw material can be 'cooked' in a sense that Pike did not intend. The 'cooking' may often be given a bogus plausibility. For instance, the English words *rib* and *rip* cannot really be considered a minimal pair because of the difference in vowel length, which can be an awkward fact for some approaches to phonological analysis. It is possible, however, to say that one can 'factor out such low-level phonetic detail'. This means no more than saying one just ignores it; but it sounds better.[9] In fact, it sounds quite respectable, for if mathematicians can 'factor out', why should phonologists not do so? But, of course, mathematicians when 'factoring out' are not simply ignoring something. (The phrase 'low-level', moreover, merely begs the question.)

No good can come of cooking accounts, even if they are only phonological accounts of sound-systems.

(Sometimes apparent misrepresentation of facts is the result of taking phonetic terms and redefining them for phonological use. I once, for example, heard a teacher in a Linguistics Department say 'we explain to students that when something is called "voiced", that does not necessarily mean that it is accompanied by vibration of the vocal cords'. This seems shocking until it is realised that a *phonological* sense of 'voiced' is being used. However, it is potentially misleading and confusing, especially to students, to do this kind of thing, and it is better avoided.)

Phonology, and especially the phoneme concept, has had considerable influence on psycholinguistics, not always for the best. Phonologists have made some rash assertions in connection with speech perception in particular. Morris Swadesh, for example, in his well-known article 'The Phonemic Principle', wrote 'The phonemes of a language are, in a sense, percepts to the native speakers of the given language, who ordinarily hear speech entirely in terms of these percepts.'[10] The statement is made with great assurance, and others have said the same thing in different ways. However, I do not know of any good evidence which would support it.

Anyway, in spite of the lack of evidence, the idea is widely assumed to be well-established. Some psychologists, certainly, have adopted it. It is found, for example, in a fairly recent paperback on psycholinguistics.[11] The author first of all has a shot at defining the phoneme, with fair success: 'The usual definition is that phonemes are the phonetic sounds needed to make distinctions between words (or more strictly between morphemes) in a particular language', and continues, familiarly enough: 'The *k* sounds in *cat* and *cool*, though different sounds phonetically, are regarded as the same phoneme because there is no case of two words which are distinguished solely by this contrast.'

So far so good, I think we can say (though 'phonetic sounds' is not a very happy phrase). However, the author goes on to write: 'The interesting thing is that to non-linguistically trained English speakers these two *k*s psychologically sound identical despite their articulatory and acoustic differences.' The word 'psychologically' is a curious word for a psychologist to use in that context; it does not seem to mean anything, though, so I think it can be ignored. These two *k*s 'sound identical', it is claimed; which is indeed an interesting thing. Or at least it would be if it were true. But *is* it true? That is not easy to find out. Before we can try to do so, it is necessary to be quite sure we know what it means.

Does it mean that if we isolate the initial stop consonants, either mechanically, by means of some sort of segment isolator, or by getting a skilled phonetician to pronounce them, then a 'non-linguistically trained English speaker' will be unable to distinguish them? It surely cannot mean that; anyone can hear the difference when the sounds are isolated – whatever, incidentally, their mother tongue may be.

It must mean, then, that once these sounds are back into the contexts of the complete words, the audible differences will disappear. This would be an auditory illusion, analogous to various optical illusions. We know, for instance, that two lines of the same length can be made to appear to be of different lengths in different visual contexts. This is the Müller-Lyer illusion, and it illustrates actually the converse effect – the same thing made to appear different; but it is an illusion demonstrating the influence of context on perception. But how are you to find out whether the auditory illusion really does take place? I doubt if the ordinary person can listen sufficiently analytically to give a reliable answer. But in any case, how are you to ask him? A question would not be at all easy to frame in intelligible and unambiguous terms, and I for one cannot think how to do it; moreover the spelling will often confuse the issue if the person is literate.

It seems to me, in fact, that this confident, impressive, and authoritative statement is meaningless. However it is not just an isolated aberration: one hears the same thing constantly in various forms. I have even heard it said that children, when acquiring the mother tongue, have to learn *not* to discriminate between allophones of the same phoneme. Another example from the same book seems quite absurd: 'There are languages that use tone as a functional phonetic feature, a whole dimension that is irrelevant and so "unheard" in English.' Is the author really claiming that English speakers cannot hear pitch variation? Surely not. And yet I cannot think what else can be intended.

Here is a similar example, this time not from a psychologist but a linguist, writing in a widely used textbook: 'The speaker of Arabic, even if phonetically untrained, differentiates with ease between the initial consonants of the English *keel* and *call*, whereas the English speaker will not normally notice the difference unless he is phonetically trained.'[12]

Obviously the purpose of this statement is to introduce the reader to the notions of allophone and phoneme. The trouble is that although it gives the impression of stating well-established and agreed facts, the statement is totally unproved. We have seen the problems connected with the alleged inability of the English speaker to notice such a difference. What about the speaker of Arabic who, it is claimed, *is* able to notice the difference? I believe that he is neither more nor less likely to do so than an English speaker.

We can guess what lies behind the claim. In classical Arabic there are two phonemes, /k/ and /q/, one a velar and the other a uvular stop;

and in English the *keel* allophone of /k/ is further forward than the *call* allophone. So the Arabic speaker, who possesses a phonological distinction in this area, can hear the difference between the two English allophones when the native English speaker cannot.

'Speaker of Arabic', however, is a vague term, and only a few speakers of Arabic possess the phoneme /q/ in their everyday speech. In any case, for those who do have it, it is quite a long way, auditorily and articulatorily, from the initial stop of *call*. Observation shows, furthermore, that Arabic speakers (with or without /q/) have more or less the same allophones for /k/, in the same environments, as English speakers do for their /k/.

One would have the same difficulty in framing questions to put to an Arabic speaker to find out if he can 'differentiate with ease' between the /k/ of *keel* and the /k/ of *call* as one would have in framing questions to find out if an English speaker finds the two sounds the same. I doubt, though, whether any questions have ever been put on the matter to either Arabic or English speakers. In other words, what is given as an established fact in this textbook is a myth.

The British tradition has always been that there are not two separate and distinct subjects, and not two different kinds of people, with different names. The tradition survives; it is affirmed by W. E. Jones and J. Laver in their Preface to their book of readings, *Phonetics in Linguistics:* 'The phonetician, and the linguist in his capacity as a phonologist, are one.'[13] All the same, I think it needs to be reaffirmed at intervals. The temptation to separate phonology from phonetics is still strong, and in some quarters here is becoming the latest fashion.

I maintain that the British tradition does *not* mean that you have two hats, either of which you can put on when you want: the cloth cap of the phonetician or the homburg of the phonologist; but that you wear both all the time – or better perhaps neither. As I said earlier, both phonetics and phonology deal with the same subject-matter, but from different points of view. Sometimes one point of view predominates, sometimes the other; but they always interpenetrate to some extent. As my late friend and colleague Angus Sinclair put it in his book *The Conditions of Knowing*, it is a matter of 'selecting and grouping in attention'. The growing tendency for phonologists to neglect, or to ignore, the general phonetic point of view is harmful to phonology and therefore to linguistics in general. Whether it is or is not true that phonology once saved the world of linguistics from the menace of over-zealous phoneticians, the time perhaps has come when phonetics should save the world of linguistics from phonology. Or rather, perhaps one should say, from phonologists.

NOTES

1. *Biographia Literaria* (1817), ed. Sampson, Cambridge: University Press, 1920, p. 48. Ch. 4.
2. *The Philosophy of Grammar*, London: George Allen and Unwin Ltd., 1924, p. 35.
3. *The Sounds of English*, Oxford at the Clarendon Press, 1908, p. 100.
4. It should be pointed out that the corresponding words in other languages did not always develop in the same way. Compare, for example, what Saussure says about *phonétique* and *phonologie* in his *Cours de linguistique générale*, p. 57 of the 1916 edition (p. 33 of Baskin's English translation).
5. *The Life and Growth of Language* sixth edn, London: N. Trübner and Co, 1889, p. 59.
6. Pp. 14, 15.
7. Householder in *Journal of Linguistics*, 1, p. 29; Lado in *Language Learning*, 3, p. 79; Fudge in *New Horizons in Linguistics*, ed. John Lyons, p. 78; Hall in Linguistics and Your Language, p. 88; Haas in *Word*, 15, p. 1.
8. *Generative Phonology*, Prentice Hall, Inc., New Jersey, 1973 p. 12.
9. Larry M. Hyman, *Phonology: Theory and Analysis*, New York: Holt, Rinehart and Winston, 1975, p. 62.
10. *Language*, 10, p. 118 (also in *Readings in Linguistics*, ed. Martin Joos, p. 32; and in *Phonology*, ed. E. C. Fudge, p. 35).
11. Judith Greene, *Psycholinguistics*, Penguin Books, 1972, pp. 45, 46.
12. E. C. Fudge, 'Phonology', in *New Horizons in Linguistics*, ed. John Lyons, Penguin Books, p. 76.
13. See p. vii.

3

Phoneme, the Concept and the Word

There are many theories of phonology current today, and many, perhaps most of them, are phoneme theories. The essence of all of them, however, is that the various speech sounds of a language represent in some way a smaller number of more abstract, or more general, entities which lie behind them (or beneath them, or above them – almost any spatial metaphor is acceptable).

The phoneme idea is first found as an explicit concept about 1880, but for a considerable time before we can find it implicit in a number of early writers on language. They may point out, for example, that some differences of sound in a language do not affect meanings; or do not have to be shown in writing; or have no reality for either speaker or hearer, by whom they are 'not felt' or 'not heard'.

An early example is J. Odell in 1806:

> When any consonant is uttered after a vowel in the same syllable, the motion, whether of the lips or tongue, which is necessary to the formation of the consonant, must cause some small variation in the distinctive modification of the vowel... But as this effect, in any particular combination, is uniform and constant, it requires no alphabetical notation.[1]

Some forty years later, A. J. Ellis writes:

> Slight differences which occur in speaking, although marked enough to form what is termed a peculiar pronunciation, are not considered sufficient to be distinguished by separate names or characters when occurring in the same language; while the same slight distinctions are often of great importance in the pronunciation of other languages. [In the former case the distinction] is not *felt* and therefore not strictly observed.[2]

About the same date, Isaac Pitman, the shorthand inventor, and close collaborator with Ellis, wrote

> the p in 'peel' is not absolutely the same letter as the p in 'pawn', but is differently modified in each case by the succeeding vowel.

Pitman gives this as an example of the

> organic changes which the letters undergo when they enter into certain combinations, [and which] should not be marked in our writing and printing.[3]

Contemporaneously, the American linguist W. D. Whitney wrote:

> It might be laid down as a general rule, that no two modes of pronunciation of a sound require to be distinguished by separate signs, unless they may and do coexist as independent sounds in the same spoken system.[4]

And next, from the most famous nineteenth-century writer on language in Britain, Max Müller:

> Our ears as well as our tongues decline to recognise distinctions which have no practical purpose, i.e. which are not connected with a real change of meaning, and the student must be careful not to lose sight of the permanent outlines of grammatical sounds behind the ever-changing play of living speech.[5]

(The contrast of 'grammatical sounds' with 'ever-changing play of living speech' anticipates Edward Sapir:

> In watching my Nootka interpreter write his language, I often had the curious feeling that he was transcribing an ideal flow of phonetic elements which he heard, inadequately from a purely objective standpoint, as the intention of the actual rumble of speech.[6])

And lastly, from the great Henry Sweet:

> Among the special vowels of any one language we must distinguish between those differences which are *distinctive*, that is, to which differences of meaning correspond, and those which are not.[7]

This is 1877, and is about as late as we can go, for the concept was made formally explicit shortly after. Sweet made a number of similar remarks in his works, but by then he was probably familiar with phoneme theory.

It is clear that the phoneme idea was only just around the corner during most of the nineteenth century. Indeed, some of those quotations are quite startlingly prophetic. The word *phoneme* could probably be introduced at some point into each one, without affecting their meaning.

All the same, the fact is that the word *phoneme* – or some equivalent technical term – is not there. We cannot have a genuine phoneme theory until we are in a position to make *explicit* the contrast between a speech-sound and something else which is *not* a speech-sound, but although related to speech-sounds, is an entity that exists on some other sort of level. We need a *word*, a technical term, for this 'something else', this other entity or thing, if we are to make the contrast explicit, a term which can then be used to clarify, codify, and classify the status of different sorts of variation between sounds.

Edward Sapir, speaking not about the phoneme concept but about concepts in general, wrote:

> The birth of a new concept is invariably foreshadowed by a more or less strained or extended use of old linguistic material; the concept does not attain to individual and independent life until it has found a distinctive linguistic embodiment. As soon as the word is at hand, we instinctively feel with something of a sigh of relief, that the concept is ours for the handling. Not until we own the symbol do we feel that we hold a key to the immediate knowledge or understanding of the concept.[8]

And Arthur Koestler paraphrases Goethe to express the same idea: 'When the mind is at sea, a new word provides a raft.'[9]

To have a concept 'phoneme', one must have the word *phoneme*, or any equivalent technical term. The philosopher John Dewey said, in his *How We Think*, that a name is a fence, a label, and a vehicle, all in one. 'Everyone', he writes, 'has experienced how learning an appropriate name for what was dim and vague cleared up and crystallized the whole matter.' This is particularly true of a well-found technical term. It is a fence: it selects and detaches a meaning from a vague blur. It is a label: it retains, registers, stores that meaning. It is a vehicle: it allows the word to travel, to be transferred to new contexts and situations.[10]

The germ of the phoneme concept, as we have seen, was clearly in the air during the nineteenth century, however 'dim and vague' it may have been, and it was being foreshadowed by the 'more or less strained or extended use of old linguistic material' – as in Whitney's 'modes of pronunciation of a sound'. By a bit of good luck, the word that was needed came along at just the right moment. It originally had nothing to do with the concept.

The word *phoneme*, or rather *phonème*, was coined, apparently, by the French phonetician, poet, and lexicographer A. Dufriche-Desgenettes (1804–?85), a founder member of the Société de

Linguistique in Paris.[11] Dufriche-Desgenettes considered that there was no satisfactory French equivalent for *speech-sound, sprachlaut*, or *phone; son du langage* being too clumsy. So he invented *phonème* to provide one (he was a great inventor of new technical terms). The term was intended to refer to vowels and consonants, in the way in which our more recent *segment* does. He used it in a paper which he gave to the Société de Linguistique on 24 May 1873, on nasal consonants, and on subsequent occasions.[12]

Phonème turned out to be a popular coinage, and several people adopted it; among them Louis Havet (who, by the way, is credited by Daniel Jones with inventing it[13]) and F. de Saussure (who has also been credited with inventing it). It is certainly due to the latter that the term became widely known outside Paris. Among writers in French, it continued to have its original meaning for a considerable time: see, for example, J. Marouzeau, *Lexique de la terminologie linguistique*, 1943. The Oxford Dictionary and the Shorter Oxford Dictionary give *phoneme* as the equivalent of *phone*.

Saussure joined the Société de Linguistique in 1876, when he was nineteen, and two years later he published his famous *Mémoire* on the primitive system of vowels in the Indo-European languages.[14] He was just twenty-one years old when it came out. It was about the last important thing he wrote, though he died thirty-five years later. The book is famous because it contains the origin of the so-called laryngeal theory of the proto-Indo-European sound system. In the book he uses the term *phonème* without defining it, but in the sense, more or less, of speech-sound, as did others in the Société. This was probably the first occasion the term was given any currency outside Paris, for the *Mémoire* was read everywhere and much admired. Henry Sweet reviewed it in 1880. It must have made the term familiar to scholars all over Europe.

The word *phonème* may have seemed a useful term to have in French, but for other people it would be just a spare word, but one which came along at just the right moment. An unexpected destiny was awaiting it.

Its destiny lay in Russia, at the University of Kazan, to be precise. The Polish linguist Baudouin de Courtenay had been teaching there since 1868 and developing his ideas on what he called *phonetic alternations*, which he felt ought to be formalised in some way. He had a student there, M. Kruszewski, another Pole, who was applying Baudouin de Courtenay's ideas to Sanskrit, to the problems of sound alternation in the Rig-Veda. In 1879 he published a book on the subject. In it he adopted the 'spare' term phoneme, gave it a new technical sense, as something to be distinguished from, and contrasted with, speech-sound, and by doing so was able to formalise Baudouin de Courtenay's theories and make his concept explicit.

Thus the technical term made widely known by Saussure's *Mémoire* and the concept developed by Baudouin de Courtenay were brought together and united by Kruszewski.

NOTES

1. *An Essay on the Elements, Accents and Prosody, of the English Language*, London, 1806, p. 9.
2. *The Alphabet of Nature*, Part 1, Bath, 1844, pp. 23, 24.
3. *The Phonotypic Journal*, 5, 1846, p. 387.
4. 'On Lepsius's Standard Alphabet', *The Journal of the American Oriental Society*, 1843, p. 329.
5. Lecture given at the Royal Institution, London, 1843: printed in *Lectures on the Science of Language*, 2, 1875, p. 128.
6. *Language*, New York, 1921, p. 58 fn; Harvest Books edn, New York, 1949, p. 56 fn.
7. *Handbook of Phonetics*, Oxford, 1877, p. 182.
8. *Language*, p. 16; Harvest Books edn, p. 17.
9. *The Roots of Coincidence*, London, 1972, p. 43.
10. *How We Think*, 1910; revised edn, from which I quote, 1933.
11. See R. F. K. Koerner in *Phonetics*, 33, 1976.
12. See Robert Godel, *Les Sources Manuscrites du Cours de Linguistique Générale de F. de Saussure*, Paris, 1957, p. 160.
13. Daniel Jones, *The History and Meaning of the Term 'Phoneme'* 1957, p. 6 fn.
14. *Mémoire sur le system primitif des voyelles dans les langues indo-européennes*, Leipzig, 1879 (the book actually appeared the year before).

4

Segments

Segment is a relative newcomer to the technical terminology of phonetics. It does not seem to have been used before the early 1940s, but from then on it began to take the place of *sound*, or *speech-sound*, though the two still coexist. It has clear advantages over *sound* because of the useful derivatives to which it can give rise, particularly the verb *to segment*, with its noun *segmentation*; and the adjective *segmental*, with its derivatives *suprasegmental, nonsegmental, autosegmental, segmentally*.

It has an advantage also in that it is not, as 'sound' is, a common word of the language, already in use in many different contexts, and unsuitable therefore to be specialised as a technical term even when made more specific in the form of *speech-sound*.

Sound, or *speech-sound*, was long felt to be unsatisfactory, and various alternatives have been put forward by linguists over the last hundred years. Among these suggestions were 'phoneme', 'phone', 'sone', 'phthong', and probably others.

Phoneme was the first of these, coined by Dufrich-Desgenettes in Paris in 1873, as recounted earlier. It was adopted by many. However, before very long it was appropriated by the Poles Kruszewski and Baudouin de Courtenay for the concept it now universally signifies. This new meaning has prevailed.

Phone is the most successful of the suggested alternatives. R. J. Lloyd, at that time Hon. Reader in Phonetics at the University College (as it then was), Liverpool, wrote in his book *Northern English* in 1899: 'Every living language possesses a limited number of spoken sounds, out of which, in varied order, all its locutions are built up, just as its printed discourse is built up of letters. The primary sounds are called its *phones*.'[1] It was a deservedly popular term and is still widely used.

Sone was a suggestion made in 1912 by the American linguist John P. Harrington. It met with no success.[2] *Phthong* was a suggestion of Dr S.W. Carruthers of Edinburgh, made in 1900 in his *Contribution to the Mechanism of Articulate Speech*,[3] for 'a constituent unit of a physiological alphabet'. He recognised, however, that 'its uncouth look' was against it.

Segment appears to date from the beginning of the 1940s. N.C. Scott in 1941 wrote in an article that 'We can analyse the spoken language into a number of segments which we call sounds.'[4] This is the earliest example I have found, but the term has since become exceedingly popular.

It might be useful to see how the word 'segment' was used before it came into linguistics. Originally it seems to have been a geometrical term applied to a section of a circle, and later also of a sphere, an ellipse or a line. But later still it came to be used of parts which are joined together to make a whole, as in an arthropod, the spinal column, an orange, a chain, for example. The whole existed before the parts in the case of an arthropod; the parts existed first, being put together to make the whole, in the case of a chain.

'To segment', therefore, has two kinds of meaning. There is 'artificial' segmentation: it is possible to cut a bit off anything, however much of a continuum it may be, as with a circle; and there is 'natural' segmentation. In the first case, we make boundaries; in the second we detect boundaries. The fundamental problem of linguistic segmentation is whether there can be a *natural* segmentation of continuous speech. If not, if speech is a continuum in which no natural segmentation is detectable, then any segmentation of it must be *artificial*. These two opposing points of view are shown in the two metaphors 'the stream of speech', on the one hand; and 'the chain of speech', on the other.

It should be noted, incidentally, that it is not the flow of speech in its entirety that is segmented. Voice quality, pitch variation, loudness variation, rhythmic characteristics, for example, are set aside first. Segmentation then takes place of what is left. Martin Joos[5] describes the phonetic analysis of speech as having two dimensions: splitting speech into simultaneous components; and cutting speech into consecutive pieces. Both operations are involved in establishing segments. The first operation is applied only up to a certain point; the second is applied to what is left. The latter gives us the segments and the former gives us the suprasegmental features.

The widespread and rapid adoption of the term *segment* is almost certainly because K.L. Pike used it in his influential and widely read *Phonetics*, 1943.[6] In it he claims that 'some type of natural segmentation of sound sequences must be discovered when even those who deny its existence use symbols which assume this division' (pp. 54, 55). Although Pike's segment is defined articulatorily, it is auditorily detected, and hearing is reflected in the symbols which represent segments. This is challenged by R.H. Stetson, who writes, with specific reference to Pike, in his *Bases of Phonology*: 'To postulate a physiological "segment" for each phonetic symbol is physiological nonsense.'[7] As J. Carnochan has said: 'It must not be taken that the divisions of a [kymograph] tracing – which are divisions in time – will correspond point for point with the letters of the systematic transcriptions placed beneath them; the letters are certainly not divisions in time.'[8]

Pike bases his phonemic theory on segments. It is by examination of the distribution in a language of its segments, embodied in symbols, that the phonemes which they represent can be deduced. (So in theory one could establish the phonemes of an unknown language from accurately transcribed texts.) This standpoint, that segments come before phonemes, is incidentally the converse of Trubetzkoy's position, that phonemes come before segments: phonemes are established from the flow of speech first, and then segments are postulated to represent them. Trubetzkoy says a word is a *gestalt*, recognised as such by the hearer, just as an acquaintance is recognised in the street by his entire appearance.[9] He quotes with approval the remark of the German psychologist Karl Bühler, that 'the phoneme is a feature on the face of the word' – a good metaphor: nose, lips, eyes are not 'segments' of a face.[10]

In contrast to Pike's view that a stretch of speech has a natural segmentation is the view that it is an indissoluble continuum, with no natural boundaries within it. This view is at least a hundred years old. It is clearly stated, for example, by Hermann Paul in his *Principien der Sprachgeschichte* in 1886.[11] The word, he says, is 'eine continuerliche reihe von unendlich vielen lauten', 'a continuous series of infinitely numerous sounds', as H.A. Strong translates it in *Principles of the History of Language*. Strong was Professor of Latin at University College, Liverpool, and he published this translation of Paul's *Principien* in 1891. As he puts it:

A real analysis of the word into its proper elements is not merely extremely difficult, but is actually impossible. A word is not a united compound of a definite number of sounds, and alphabetical symbols do no more than bring out certain characteristic points of this series in an imperfect way. [p.39]

One wonders if Strong's Liverpool colleague R.J. Lloyd had read this when he wrote that all locutions are built up of phones 'just as printed discourse is made up of letters'.

Earlier Henry Sweet had anticipated this standpoint. His *Handbook of Phonetics*, 1877, has two main parts, one entitled 'Analysis' and the other entitled 'Synthesis'.[13] Analysis regards 'each sound...as if it were a fixed isolated element', 'a fixed stationary point', whereas Synthesis regards it 'as a momentary point in a stream of incessant change'. Analysis deals with a momentary point *as if* it were a fixed, isolated element. To operate with something *as if* it was something else is to operate with a fiction.

The monumental *Philosophy of 'As If'*, by Hans Vaihinger, shows how common such fictions are in a variety of fields.[14] For some people there is something discreditable about using a fiction in scientific work, though 'fiction', of course, is a neutral technical term.

R.T. Butlin, in a paper read to the Philological Society in 1937, said that many of the disputes of phonetic theorists and phonologists arose because much of what was both stoutly maintained, and vigorously assailed, as a matter of observed fact, was, it should be realised, a body of practically convenient fictions. As he said, the fiction, consciously and deliberately used for a definite purpose, is the most sophisticated of scientific devices.[15]

Segment, then, is the name of a fiction. It is a transient moment treated *as if* it was frozen in time, put together with other segments to form a 'chain' rather than a 'stream' of speech. Methodologically it is a very useful fiction. A segment, isolated from the flow of speech, can be taken out of its context, moved into other contexts, given a symbol to represent it, compared with segments from other languages, placed in systems of various sorts, singled out for special treatment in pronunciation teaching; and used in dialectology, speech therapy, the construction of orthographies. (The same is true, of course, of speechsound and phone. They do not give rise, however, to the possibility of a word for the *process*, 'segmentation'.)

Eventually, of course, the continuum must be reconstituted. This is done by the introduction of *glides*, another fiction whose only function is to join segments together. The glide is an example of what is known as the *antithetic error*. Two wrongs here make a right.

There is always a danger of hypostatising a fiction. The tendency to attribute reality to a segment is a tendency which is reinforced by the letters of phonetic transcription, or of alphabetic writing. It has often seemed to me that the Chinese, who have an ideographic script, when learning to pronounce English, with its alphabetic script, are not tempted to attribute independent reality to entities symbolised by letters. And the 'look-and-say' method of teaching children to read treats the word as a whole, as a *gestalt*, unlike the 'phonic' method, which arrives at the word via successive segments.

Pike's *Phonetics* postulates the existence of a 'nonfictitious' phonetic segmentation (see p. 4); he declared (p. 47) it to be a fact that a universal segmentation lies behind vocal expression. His invaluable and exhaustive account of the speech-producing mechanisms, including the part they play in producing non-speech sounds, would be rendered in no way invalid by acknowledging that a segment is a fiction.

The segment is an invaluable methodological fiction, but it is not an indispensable one. Not to recognise or admit its fictitious nature does little harm to phonetic analysis or description, but it prevents one from seeing that other approaches to analysis and description are possible, and for some purposes preferable. A segmental basis is not the most satisfactory way of making synthetic speech, for example; and the whole of Firthian phonology is based on quite different fictions.

NOTES

1. *Northern English,* Leipzig, 1899; 2nd edn 1908. p. 1.
2. 'Notes on certain usages relating to linguistic work', *American Anthropologist,* 14, p. 186.
   The terms 'sone', 'sonetic', 'soneme' were used by Sylvia Broadbent in 1987, when discussing the 'reconstitution' of languages no longer spoken but of which old vocabulary lists and texts are still available. See *International Journal of American Linguistics,* 22, p. 273.
3. Originally appeared in the *Edinburgh Medical Journal* in three parts, in September, October, and November 1900. Carruthers thought 'phone' was 'a more genteel word', and used it in preference to 'phthong'. See my 'Direct palatography', *Zeitschrift für Phonetik,* 10, 1957, pp. 21-5; reprinted in *Studies in Phonetics and Linguistics,* Oxford University Press, 1965.
4. 'Broad transcription', *Maître Phonétique,* 1941, p. 48.
5. Martin Joos, *Acoustic Phonetics,* Supplement to *Language,* 24, 1948, p. 98.

32 *Segments*

6. *Phonetics: A Critical Analysis of Phonetic Theory and a Technic for the Practical Description of Sounds*, Ann Arbor: University of Michigan Press; lithoprinted edn, in which a few misprints are corrected, 1944.
7. R. H. Stetson, *Bases of Phonology*, Oberlin College, Ohio, 1945.
8. *Bulletin of the School of Oriental and African Studies*, 12, part 2, 1948, p. 426.
9. N. S. Trubetzkoy, *Grundzüge der Phonologie*, Prague, 1939, p. 34. Gestalt is rendered by 'silhouette' in J. Cantineau's translation of Trubetzkoy, *Principes de Phonologie*, Paris, Klincksieck, 1949. p. 38. Christiane A. M. Baltaxe's translation, *Principles of Phonology*, Berkeley and Los Angeles: University of California Press, 1969, renders this as 'each word is a phonic entity, a *gestalt*' p. 35.
10. So Bühler's aphorism is often translated. His actual words were, as quoted by Trubetzkoy, 'Lautmal am Wortkörper' (p. 39) or 'Lautmal am Wortgesicht' (p. 40).
11. Hermann Paul, *Principien der Sprachgeschichte, zweite Auflage*, Halle: Max Niemeyr, 1886; see p. 48.
12. *Principles of the History of Language by Hermann Paul*, translated from the second edn. of the original by H. A. Strong, professor of Latin in University College, Liverpool. New and revised edn, London: Longmans, Green, and Co., 1891.
13. Henry Sweet, *A Handbook of Phonetics, Including a Popular Exposition of the Principles of Spelling Reform*, Oxford, 1877; reprinted Maryland: McGrath Publishing Co., 1970. Sweet's *Primer of Phonetics*, 1892; 2nd edn, revised, 1902; 3rd edn, revised, 1906, has the same division into two parts, explained in the same way.
14. Hans Vaihinger, *The Philosophy of 'As If', A System of the Theoretical, Practical and Religious Fictions of Mankind*, translated by C. K. Ogden, London: Kegan Paul, Trench, Trübner and Co., 1924.
15. A summary of the paper was printed in *Transactions of the Philological Society*, 1937, p. 137.

Postscript: Since this chapter was in type, I have been reminded that Hermann Paul had been anticipated some fifty years before by Karl Ferdinand Becker, in his *Ausführliche deutsche Grammatik*, (Frankfort-am-Main, 1836). Becker contended that a word is an 'undivided unit, which cannot properly be said to be *compounded* of several others, as a *written* word is of letters', to quote A. J. Ellis's rendering in his *Alphabet of Nature* (Part I, Bath, 1844), pp. 19, 20. ('Das Wort tritt in der lebendigen Sprache ursprünglich als ungetheilte Einheit hervor; es wird nicht eigentlich *zusammengesetzt* aus Lauten, wie etwa das *geschriebene* Wort aus Buchstaben.') It is highly likely that Paul was acquainted with Becker's Grammar.

5

Hylomorphic Taxonomy and William Holder

Published in *Journal of the International Phonetic Association* Vol. 16, pp. 4-7, 1986

The 'hylomorphic' distinction between *matter* and *form* was the basis, for many seventeenth-century writers, of the analysis of the sound of speech. *Matter* was breath, to which *form* was given by articulations of the organs of speech. This theory of matter and form, hylomorphic theory, was derived from Aristotle, and in the Middle Ages came to be used in many different fields. Its application to the taxonomy of the sounds of speech, or letters, is one of the most recent.

Matter, for many writers, was considered to be not just breath alone, but to be two-fold, being breath *and* voice. As William Holder (1616-98), for example, puts it in his *Elements of Speech: An Essay of Inquiry into the Natural Production of Letters,* 1669: 'Of *Letters* the *Material* part is *Breath* and *Voice*: the *Formal* part is constituted by the *Motions* and *Figures* of the *Organs* of *Speech*.' Or to take another example, from Dr John Conrad Amman, in the translation of his *Surdus Loquens* in 1694 by Dr Daniel Foot under the title *The Talking Deaf Man*: 'I shall bring into examination *First*, the material part of the *Letters*, viz. *Voice* and *Breath*.'

Holder points out that 'it is one thing to *Breath*, or give an impulse to breath alone; another thing, to *Vocalise* that breath, i.e. in its passage through the larynx to give it the sound of Humane Voyce'.

The mechanism by which breath is vocalised was not properly understood in the seventeenth century. It was known that voice somehow had its origin in the larynx (or, as some put it less precisely, in the throat); but the role of the vocal cords, for which incidentally there was as yet no name, was not known.

Holder comes much closer to the truth than anyone else before him: 'The Larynx both gives *Passage* to the breath, and also, as often as we please, by the force of Muscles, to bear the sides of the Larynx stiffe and near together, as the Breath passeth through the Rimula, makes a vibration of those cartilaginous Bodies [i.e., the sides of the larynx] which forms that Breath, into a Vocal sound or Voice' (*Rimula*, diminutive of *rima*, means chink or narrow orifice; here evidently it is equivalent to *glottis*.)

As a matter of fact, as far as the analysis and description of spoken language are concerned, ignorance of the true mechanism of phonation does not matter very much. However, it was not just the mechanism of phonation that was not understood; the role that it plays in consecutive speech was for the most part unclear, and that was a more serious matter. It was obvious, of course, that it is responsible for the pitch variation in speech; but the fact that voice accompanies some stretches of speech and not others, phonation being continually turned off and on as it were, was not properly understood.

Holder is perfectly clear. He says of [p] and [b] that one is 'an Articulation of *Breath*, the other of *Voice*', and they are described as *spiral* and *vocal*, respectively. Holder therefore envisaged the possibility of such voiceless consonants as [m̥ n̥ ŋ̊ l̥ r̥] – consonants which many people rashly maintained could not exist.

Holder, however, introduces an important refinement to the theory: for him the matter of speech is fourfold. Although 'Of *Letters* the *material* part is *Breath* and *Voice*', a further 'material discrimination' is afforded by the nose 'sometimes giving passage to Breath or Voice'. The material part, therefore, is either *breath* or *voice*, but it is also either *oral* or *nasal*. The application of these two separate dichotomies thus yields four kinds of matter: ore-spiral, ore-vocal, naso-spiral, and naso-vocal.

Holder was alone in thus postulating a fourfold matter, but for many seventeenth-century writers there was nevertheless a category *nasal* (not, curiously enough, for all).

There is less of a problem in understanding the difference between oral and nasal than there was with breath and voice: the physiological process involved is more amenable to observation. Nevertheless, some failed to recognise the role played by the soft palate in opening up and shutting off the nasal cavity. However, it was fairly common knowledge that the 'uvula' acted as a valve (neither the term *soft palate* nor *velum (palati)* were used by writers on phonetics until the late eighteenth century, and *uvula* must be taken before that to be the equivalent term).

Since for Holder the difference between *nasal* and *oral* belongs to *matter* and not *form*, when the material part of speech is naso-vocal, it can be 'discriminated' by *any* articulatory movement. He did not limit his consideration of nasality, therefore, as did nearly all other writers of the time, to the nasal consonants [m n ŋ].

He has in his book a consonant chart showing four elements or letters for each articulation. Thus the articulation 'labial' gives rise to (in IPA notation) [p b m̥m]; 'gingival' to [t d ņ n]; 'palatick' to [k g ŋ̊ ŋ]; 'gingival-sibilant' to [s z š ž]; 'gingival-jarring' to [ɽ r ř̥ ř]; and so on. Needless to say, John Martyn, Printer to the Royal Society, who published the book, could not provide characters for most of the consonants appearing on the chart. Holder indicates where characters are missing by prefixing an 'obelisk' to a traditional character. As pointed out by Holder, many of the missing characters are unlikely ever to be needed.

Not placed on the chart are two more consonants which he mentions, namely [h] and [ʔ], 'the Stop made by closing the Larynx'.

The application of hylomorphic theory to the taxonomy of speech sounds is essentially a seventeenth-century phenomenon. Before that, although the theory of matter and form was doubtless well known, it had not occurred to any one that it could be applied to speech. However, once it was adopted it made a considerable contribution to seventeenth-century phonetics.

As the eighteenth century began interest in phonetics died down, and it did not revive for quite some time, until the last quarter of the century in fact. By this time hylomorphic theory had been forgotten, but its influence on taxonomy may be said to have endured to the present day.

Dr William Holder's *Elements of Speech* is a treatise on general phonetics, with special reference to the teaching of the deaf. It is not 'an attempt to describe scientifically the sounds of English', as the prefatory note to The Scholar Press reprint alleges.

The word 'element' in the title has the same meaning as the more commonly used 'letter'. It means here 'the fundamental units of', and not 'the rudiments of' as it does in many modern titles, including my own *Elements of General Phonetics*.

Dr William Holder lived a long, useful, and respected life. He was considered to be a man of kind and equable temperament, and his career for the most part was free of quarrels in what was a very quarrelsome era – except that he did not escape an acrimonious controversy with one of the most quarrelsome men of that time, John Wallis.

Among his many other accomplishments William Holder was an expert writer of shorthand. The system he used was the one invented by Theophilus Metcalfe (1610–1646?), and sometimes called radio stenography. It was first published about 1635. It was one of the most popular of the seventeenth-century shorthands. A manuscript of the entire Bible transcribed by Dr Holder into Metcalfe's system is in the British Library.

John Aubrey, the antiquarian whose *Brief Lives* are a source of so much information (and gossip) about men and women of the seventeenth century, wrote of Dr Holder: 'He is a handsome, graceful person, and of a delicate constitution, and of an even and smooth temper; so that, if one would goe about to describe a perfect good man, would draw this Doctor's character' (1949, p. 160).

REFERENCES

D. Abercrombie, *Elements of General Phonetics*, Edinburgh: Edinburgh University Press, 1967.

J. C. Amman, *The Talking Deaf Man: Or, a Method Proposed, Whereby He who is Born Deaf May Learn to Speak*, imprinted at Amsterdam, by Henry Westein, 1692, and now done out of Latin into English by Daniel Foot, M.D. London, 1694.

J. Aubrey, *Brief Lives*, edited from the original manuscript and with an introduction by Oliver Lawson Dick, London: Secker and Warburg, 1949.

W. Holder, *Elements of Speech: An Essay of Inquiry into the Natural Production of Letters*, London: printed by T. N. for J. Martyn, printer to the Royal Society, at the Bell without Temple-Barr, 1669, reprinted in 1967 as a Scolar Press Facsimile, Menston: The Scholar Press.

6

Daniel Jones's Teaching

Daniel Jones Memorial Lecture, given at Leeds University, 18 March 1982.
Circulated privately in *Work in Progress* No. 15, 1982. Published in *Phonetic
Linguistics*, Essays in Honor of Peter Ladefoged, Ed. Victoria A. Fromkin,
Academic Press Inc., Orlando, Florida, 1985

I feel most honoured to be asked to give this Daniel Jones Memorial
Lecture, and I am grateful to be given this opportunity to pay tribute to
a great phonetician and one of the most influential figures in British
linguistics. I met Daniel Jones over fifty years ago, and continued to be
in touch with him until he died in 1967, at the age of eighty-six.

I would like to take a look at some of the points that characterised his
teaching, and particularly at points which are controversial but which
have been influential in the development of linguistics in this country
– though the importance of some of them is in danger of being
forgotten nowadays. Jones was not a profound thinker, and he did not
pretend to be; nevertheless he was an outstanding teacher, demanding
but kind; and his teaching left an indelible impression on all who
passed through his hands.

Let me start, though, by recounting how I first came to meet Jones,
and as a consequence, rather unexpectedly, became his student; and
eventually, I think I may say, his friend. At the time when I met him I
was a postgraduate student here at the University of Leeds. I was
registered for an M.A. in the English Department, but after completing
my first degree I had gone to live with my parents in London. The thesis
topic on which I was working was 'The Phonetic Basis of i-Mutation',
under the supervision of E.V. Gordon, author of *An Introduction to Old
Norse*. I spent my time in London working in the Reading Room of the
British Museum.

My father and Daniel Jones knew each other because they were both
members of the BBC Advisory Committee on Spoken English. My
father told Jones one day that he had a son who was very interested in
phonetics, and Jones very kindly suggested that I should go and have

a talk with him. So I made an appointment, and went one October morning in 1930 to Jones's house in Golders Green. I think I was expecting to have an informal discussion which would give me some guidance about how an aspiring young phonetician, doing an M.A. in English Language, should plan his future in the academic world. However, it did not turn out like that at all. Jones answered the door himself, let me in, and said 'How do you do? Come in and sit down. Would you please say a voiced bilabial implosive?' At that time I was not aware that he did not have much in the way of small talk. Fortunately I was able to produce the required implosive, and he then said 'Thank you. Now will you please say a close back unrounded vowel.' As it happened I could do so, and did; and the rigorous performance examination went on for some time. He put no theoretical questions to me at all. But eventually he said he thought I should not worry too much about my Leeds M.A., but that I should right away become a student in his Department at University College. I followed his recommendation. I continued working at my thesis, but I was also a postgraduate student at University College over a period of seven years, during two of which I was also working at the Institut de Phonétique in Paris. They were probably the happiest days of my life; but I never got my M.A. finished.

Jones as a phonetician belonged to a tradition, one which still continues, and one which goes back a long way: a tradition of teaching methods, of descriptive techniques, of technical terminology, of notation, handed on from one generation to the next. Phoneticians in this tradition were brought up by other phoneticians; few phoneticians in this country have been self-taught. Jones's predecessors included Ellis, Bell, and Sweet, and many phoneticians in Europe such as Storm, Passy, Viëtor, Jespersen. This is in remarkable contrast with America. It was possible for G.L. Trager to say, in 1943: 'Phonetics is so young a branch of science that it is still true that most phoneticians are self-taught.'[1] It would have been unthinkable to say such a thing in 1943 here; but it was true of America.

It is not easy to see why a tradition did not establish itself in America, as it did here. After all, they had a fine phonetician who was contemporary with our founding fathers, Ellis and Bell: S.S. Haldeman (1812–80), author of *Analytic Orthography*, 1860, a paper on phonetic notation. Originally a geologist, he became the first Professor of Comparative Philology at the University of Pennsylvania. (Daniel Jones used to say that the only discipline with which phonetics had nothing at all in common was geology.) He published on Indian and many other languages, and became a fine self-taught phonetician, of whom Ellis and Bell thought highly. And there were others who might have started a tradition, including Alexander Melville Bell himself, who became an American citizen, and his son Alexander Graham Bell.

Jones was a superb teacher, and his staff in the Department were all superb teachers. Great importance was attached in the Department's teaching to *performance* – which perhaps explains the nature of my preliminary interview with Jones. *General* phonetics as such was hardly ever taught. Students were taught the pronunciation of specific languages; matters of general theory were discussed only if they arose in connection with these. The languages whose pronunciation was taught were very varied phonologically, and provided a broad survey of human phonetic capabilities. Among the languages on whose pro- nunciation I had to work, I remember, were Urdu, German, Sechuana, Cantonese, Sinhalese, Russian, and Danish, and I expect others. In addition, of course, to French – everybody in the Department had to do French. In all these the very highest standards of performance were demanded of the students.

This way of teaching phonetics meant intensive training of the proprioceptive, i.e. the tactile and kinesthetic, senses concerned with the organs of speech, something that is not valued very highly by many other schools of phonetics. The proprioceptive senses, in the view of phoneticians in the Jones tradition, play an important part in the analysis and description of unfamiliar sounds. The phonetician, having learnt to make a sound of the language he is working on to the complete satisfaction of his native informant, then examines what he himself is doing with his vocal organs, and infers the informant is doing he same thing. I have met many phoneticians, both in America and on the Continent, who are not capable of doing this; who believe, in fact, that there is something wrong with it as a procedure. It has been called (by a postgraduate student at Edinburgh University) 'analysis by perform- ance'. However, there was one topic of general phonetics which was taught in Jones's Department, and that was the system of Cardinal Vowels.

The system of Cardinal Vowels constitutes a technique, not a theory. It is a technique of description, a technique for providing much more precise specifications of vowels than the traditional kind of taxonomic approach is able to do. It is a technique that is not used in America, and not much used by Continental phoneticians; it belongs more or less exclusively to the British tradition, though, as we know, it was adopted by the IPA. The *idea* of cardinal vowels was put forward by Ellis, the *word* 'cardinal' by Bell, and Henry Sweet, too, spoke of 'cardinal vowel positions'. But only Daniel Jones produced a fully worked-out system. Sweet said that phonetics is both a science and an art. It should be remembered that the Cardinal Vowel technique belongs to the art, and not to the science, side of the subject.

It is a technique which is time-consuming and difficult to learn. I was taught the Cardinal Vowels by Jones himself, and it was a lengthy and painful process. Cardinal Vowel Number One turned out to be the most difficult of all, rather unexpectedly, and it took a long time before Jones was satisfied with my version. I had trouble, too, with Cardinal Number Three, I remember. Once I had learnt the Cardinal Vowels from Jones, other members of staff, and especially Ida Ward, later to become Professor of African Languages in London University, taught me how to use them as a descriptive technique.

Recently, cardinal vowels have been the object of much criticism, arising from a widespread misunderstanding of how they should be used in description. I was taught to use them proprioceptively, and I think that is how everyone used them at the time. With practice, it is true, one learns to take short cuts from the auditory impression straight to the placing of the dot on the Cardinal Vowel figure, the trapezium. But the full procedure was to imitate the informant until one had the vowel perfect, and then to feel, by means of the tactile and kinesthetic senses, how the tongue posture compared with that of the nearest Cardinal Vowels, and the identifying dot on the figure was placed accordingly. The lip posture had to be stated separately, but it is, after all, easy enough to see.

Nowadays, however, it is claimed by many people that the Cardinal Vowel figure encloses, not an articulatory space, but an *auditory* space. In other words, a dot placed on the figure represents, not a tongue position, but a quality of sound. The difficulty of this view, though, is that some of this quality of sound must derive from the posture of the lips, which varies independently of the tongue posture; yet the two-dimensional space of the Cardinal Vowel figure cannot accommodate what in effect are three variables affecting vowel quality. Hence the criticism that the set of eight Cardinal Vowels should not be a mixture of vowels with lip-rounding and vowels without. A curiously angry article on this subject appeared some while ago in the *Journal of the International Phonetic Association*.[2] It said that the fact that some Cardinal Vowels are rounded while others are unrounded means the system contains 'a contradiction so basic that any attempt to make use of it as a descriptive technique would be completely impossible'. It is not explained how such a basic contradiction has escaped attention until now, nor how it is that the system has been used successfully as a descriptive technique during the last seventy or so years.

However, there is only a contradiction if it is supposed that the Cardinal Vowel figure represents an auditory space, and that vowels are placed on it auditorily. I do not know when and where such an idea started, but it is now quite widespread. It is to be found, for example, in J.D. O'Connor's Pelican *Phonetics*, 1973.

It follows that if one wishes to relate a speaker's vowels to the Cardinal Vowels, it is necessary to be able to *see* him: one needs to know what his lips are doing. Peter Ladefoged conducted an interesting and well-known experiment[3] to investigate how well phoneticians would agree with each other in placing the vowels of a number of test-words in an unknown language on the Cardinal Vowel figure. On the whole, they did pretty well. But this particular language contained some unrounded back vowels of varying degrees of closeness, and on these agreement was rather poor. However, it must be noted that it was not a live informant that was being used in the experiment; the judgements were made from recordings. If the speaker's lip-posture had been visible, the tongue positions might have been judged very much more accurately. The same consideration applies to another interesting experiment, carried out by John Laver, designed to test how consistent individual phoneticians were at assessing vowels over periods of time. Again, recordings were used, and moreover recordings which were of synthetic, not humanly produced, vowels.[4]

There have been suggestions recently that the time has now come to produce a new set of Cardinal Vowels, or perhaps a new Cardinal Vowel figure. But there would be a problem in getting a new system generally accepted, and getting it consistently taught; there seems little chance of a successful attempt. Some new figures have been put forward, but they do not seem to have caught on.

A curious criticism concerns the division of Cardinal Vowels into 'primary' and 'secondary'. No vowel, it is claimed, can be more primary than any other; all vowels are equal. I am sure there were no *theoretical* reasons for singling out some vowels rather than others. The eight primary Cardinal Vowels were ones which Jones said he found to be 'convenient' and 'in practice to give particularly good results'. They are primary (though he never used that term for them, as I remember), only in that he established them first. The secondary (or 'subsidiary' as he originally called them) Cardinal Vowels he thought of later. Jones was a bit vague about their exact purpose (there are now ten; originally there were fourteen). I do not remember them being used by anyone in descriptions. Jones, it is true, made a recording of them; but he did not teach them, as far as I know – certainly not to me anyway.

As a matter of fact, in principle, almost any set of vowels could form a system of Cardinal Vowels. The only requirement is that they should be conveniently situated within the vowel area to act as location points. They do not have to be easy to learn: they are to be used by professional phoneticians, who are supposed to be able to learn anything. But once the vowels are decided on, they must thereafter be fixed and invariable, or they will not work as a technique of description.

Many people would think, though, that a system of Cardinal Vowels provides much more accuracy as a descriptive technique than is needed for most purposes. I am inclined to think so myself. The traditional taxonomic categories are normally good enough.

However, the Cardinal Vowels have another use in addition to providing a descriptive technique: they provide an excellent basis for exercises for beginners in phonetics, as target points for practice in performance classes. In such exercises absolute perfection of perform-ance is not insisted on, as it must be if the vowels are being taught as a descriptive technique. And here the secondary Cardinal Vowels come into their own: they too are excellent for practice for beginners.

One of Jones's chief interests throughout his career was notation, with which he experimented a great deal. He worked out in 1907, for example, together with Paul Passy, an 'Organic Phonetic Alphabet'. It was perhaps meant to rival Sweet's Organic Alphabet, itself derived from Alexander Melville Bell's Visible Speech. In all these the shapes of the letters were intended to be self-interpreting. Jones and Passy published their alphabet as a supplement to the *Maître Phonétique* at the end of 1907, but it was hardly ever heard of again. I never heard Jones talk about it. Jones was also a very keen advocate of the reform of English spelling, and he was an influential member of the Simplified Spelling Society, of which, for a time, he was President. After the last war he went so far as to write all his personal correspondence in Nue Speling. Another of his notational interests was the problem of a roman-based national script for India (it was an interest also of J.R. Firth, and this was one of the few points on which they collaborated).

His best-known interest, however, was in the notation of the International Phonetic Association, and in different types of transcription making use of it. He had much to do with making the IPA alphabet widely used throughout the world. He took an especial interest in types of transcription of English. He made famous one type of transcription which was used in many of his books, and especially in all but the most recent edition of the *English Pronouncing Dictionary*; it is often in consequence called 'the Jones transcription of English'. However, it was not Jones who devised it; it was the way English was transcribed by many members of the IPA at the time that Jones became a member in 1905. It was the type of transcription used in the *Phonetic Dictionary of the English Language*, by Hermann Michaelis and Daniel Jones, the second in a series of phonetic dictionaries under the general editorship of Michaelis. It came out in 1913, and in it the words are arranged according to their pronunciation, the orthography coming afterwards. It was natural, when Jones came to make his own more orthodox pronouncing dictionary four years later, to continue with the same type of transcription. I have heard Jones say, though, that he did not really like it.

But although what is often said to be *the* Jones transcription of English is in fact not his, he did work out several other types of transcription for English. There was, for example, the type he called 'extra broad', which has been used by a number of phoneticians in their books, for example by N.C. Scott, E.L. Tibbitts, and others; and, in a slightly modified form, by P.A.D. MacCarthy. There was the so-called 'narrow' transcription which Miss I.C. Ward and Miss L.E. Armstrong used in their various books, and which proved popular with many other writers. Jones made several other experiments in the transcription of English.

Like a number of other people in the IPA early this century, Jones attached great importance to the general appearance and, above all, to the legibility of the printed page, and in consequence he believed great care should be taken over the design of letter shapes. It was ensured that new symbols added to the alphabet were typographically satisfactory; suggested symbols that were unsatisfactory were not officially accepted. For example, the absence in the IPA alphabet of distinct symbols for voiceless nasals, instead of using the symbols for voiced nasals with a devoicing diacritic added, has been taken by some to be theoretically motivated. It is claimed the IPA has assumptions of 'normality' and 'abnormality' as regards sounds, and that the use of the diacritic shows the sound is regarded as 'abnormal', a voiced nasal being more 'normal'.[5] But the IPA has no such assumptions and conventions, and never has had. The plain fact is that no typographically acceptable symbols for voiceless nasals have yet been put forward, though there have been many suggestions. I do not think the IPA has ever allowed contentious theoretical considerations – or rival phonological analyses – to influence its choice of symbols.

Jones's concern for typographical appearance is illustrated by the length of time that his book on *The Phoneme* took to appear after he had finished writing it. It is said that he considered the dot over the i in the Gill Sans typeface, which he was using in the book for phonetic notation, was too high above the stem, and time had to be spent on re-cutting it. It must be admitted, however, that the first two editions of his *Pronunciation of English*, 1909 and 1914, were typographically hideous: at that date I do not think he was able to impose his will on his publishers as he could later.

In America phonetic notation has had a curious history. Bloomfield used IPA notation in his early book *An Introduction to the Study of Language*, 1914, and in the English edition of his more famous *Language*, 1935. But since then, a strange hostility has been shown by many American linguists to IPA notation, especially to certain of its symbols.

An interesting and significant story was once told by Carl Voegelin during a symposium held in New York in 1952 on the present state of anthropology. He told how, at the beginning of the 1930s, he was being taught phonetics by, as he put it, a 'pleasant Dane', who made him use the IPA symbol for *sh* in *ship*, among others. Some while later he used those symbols in some work on an American Indian language he had done for Sapir. When Sapir saw the work he 'simply blew up', Voegelin said, and demanded that in future Voegelin should use 's wedge' (as š was called), instead of the IPA symbol.[6]

I have no doubt that the 'pleasant Dane' was H. J. Uldall, one of Jones's most brilliant students, who was later to become one of the founders of glossematics, with Louis Hjelmslev. Uldall did a great deal of research into Californian languages, especially into Maidu or Nisenan. Most of the texts he collected were not published during his lifetime. It is ironic that when they were published, posthumously, by the University of California Press, the texts were 'reorthographised', as the editor's introduction put it: the IPA symbols Uldall had used were removed and replaced by others.[7]

What is strange is that the IPA symbols seem so obviously preferable to the Americanist alternatives, the 'long s' to the 's wedge', for example. As Jones often pointed out, in connected texts, for the sake of legibility diacritics should be avoided as far as possible. Many Americanist texts give the impression of being overloaded with diacritics.

One may wonder why there should be such hostility in America to IPA notation. I venture to suggest a reason for this apparently irrational attitude. The hostility derives ultimately from the existence, in most American universities, of Speech Departments, which we do not have in Britain. Speech Departments tend to be well-endowed, large, and powerful. In linguistic and phonetic matters they have a reputation for being predominantly prescriptive, and tend to be considered by some therefore to be not very scholarly. In their publications and periodicals the notation they use, when writing of pronunciation, is that of the IPA. My belief is that the last thing a member of an American Linguistics Department wants is to be mistaken for a member of a Speech Department; but if he were to use IPA notation in his writings he would certainly lay himself open to the suspicion that he was.

The phoneme is a topic with which Jones was greatly concerned, and I think he was disappointed that people did not have more regard for what he had to say on the subject. His writings on the phoneme met with little respect in America – and little respect even in parts of his own Department. In a paper[8] that I gave a while ago I recounted how, when I first went to the Department, I found it was divided, geographically and ideologically, into two parts: upstairs and downstairs. Upstairs was Daniel Jones and most of the lecturers. Downstairs, in the basement, was the laboratory, presided over by Stephen Jones (no relation) and much frequented by J.R. Firth and various postgraduate students. Downstairs was, on the whole, fairly critical of upstairs. While admiring the expertise in practical phonetics to be found upstairs, downstairs thought the lack of interest in general theoretical matters upstairs to be deplorable. Jones's phoneme concept had the minimum of theory behind it. Jones always said there was no such thing as phonology as a subject separate from phonetics (he never used the word phonemics). His phoneme concept was unpretentious and unadventurous. Its purpose was to be of service to applied phonetics, especially the making of transcriptions for language teaching. As Jones wrote[9] in 1931: 'The main object of grouping the sounds of a language into phonemes is to establish a simple and adequate way of writing the language.' Nothing more ambitious was expected of the concept. Jones took the idea of the phoneme in 1911 from the Russian phonetician Ščerba, as is well known.

The idea, Jones has said, began to find a 'regular place' in his Department's teaching from 1915. It underwent very little development afterwards.

By contrast, the phoneme idea came relatively late to America. In 1934 Morris Swadesh wrote: 'It is only quite recently that the phonemic principle has had the serious attention of linguists.'[10] As a matter of fact the phonemic principle might have had attention in America very much earlier, for a now largely-forgotten linguist, J.P. Harrington, adumbrated it in 1912. He proposed the adoption into English of the word 'phonem' (without an 'e' at the end), and he wrote that in the language of the Tewa Pueblo Indians, *ng* and *g*, for example, are 'two aspects of the same phonem, as is the case with Castilian *g* and levis *g*, *d* and levis *d, b,* and levis *b*'. Unfortunately nobody followed his suggestion, perhaps because although he was known as a talented phonetician and gifted fieldworker, he was also a noted eccentric. Nevertheless, he himself continued to use his term all his working life.[11]

Incidentally, the form 'phonem' is not found in the O.E.D., even though others besides Harrington have used it, sometimes as a different word from 'phoneme': see, for instance, G.E. Fuhrken, *Standard English Speech* (Cambridge University Press,1932) where 'phonem' is defined as 'one sound or a series of sounds forming a connected whole', whereas 'phoneme' is 'a sound and its varieties in one and the same language'.

I was one of the sceptics in the Department as far as the 'upstairs' phoneme and its objectives were concerned. Conversation downstairs in the laboratory was apt to make fun of the 'joneme', which was not very difficult to do. I have now come rather to admire it, and to think it has applications beyond applied phonetics. I have come to think, after experimenting in various ways, that it provides, in teaching general phonetics to beginners, the best foundation on which to base consideration of phonology in general.

A remarkable expansion of linguistics in British universities took place after the war, and phoneticians trained in the Jones tradition played an important part in the foundation and development of many new departments. This success story may now be coming to an end. The whole academic world is under threat, I know; but it may be that linguistics and phonetics are among the more vulnerable subjects. The rapid growth in recent years of linguistics and phonetics has meant that there are a large number of departments in Britain – too many, some may think; and it is likely that in some quarters it will be felt that some departments are expendable. Already in Scotland, we hear, the Departments at St Andrews and at Glasgow are to be closed shortly. Chairs and vacant lectureships are not being filled – as, indeed, in other Departments. A short list of applicants was established for my Chair, when I retired, but it did not get as far as an appointment being made. I am sad to finish on such a despondent note, but I feel sure there will be a considerable shrinkage of linguistics in the academic world in the near future. Let us hope that the invaluable tradition consolidated and transmitted by Daniel Jones will nevertheless be preserved.

NOTES

1. In a review of K. L. Pike's *Phonetics* in *Studies in Linguistics,* 2, 1943, p. 16.
2. J. Derrick McClure, 'A suggested revision for the Cardinal Vowel system', *Journal of the International Phonetic Association,* 2, June 1972, pp. 20-5.
3. 'The value of phonetic statements', *Language,* 36, July–September 1960, pp. 387–96; also ch. 2 of *Three Areas of Experimental Phonetics,* London, 1967.
4. J. D. M. H. Laver, 'Variability in vowel perception', *Language and Speech,* 8, April–June, 1965, pp. 95–121.
5. See, for example, John Lyons, *Introduction to Theoretical Linguistics,* Cambridge, 1968, ch. 3.
6. *An Appraisal of Anthropology Today,* ed. Sol Tax *et al.,* Chicago: University of Chicago Press, 1966.
7. *Nisenan Texts and Dictionary,* by H. J. Uldall and W. Shipley, Berkeley: University of California Press, 1966.
8. *Work in Progress,* No. 13, Department of Linguistics, University of Edinburgh, 1980; reprinted in *Forum Linguisticum,* 5, 1980.
9. 'On phonemes', *Travaux du Cercle Linguistique de Prague,* 4, Prague, 1931, pp. 74–9.
10. 'The phonemic principle', *Language,* 10, 1934, pp. 117–29.
11. John Peabody Harrington (1884–1961) spent most of his career working for the Bureau of American Ethnology at the Smithsonian Institution, specialising in the Indian languages of California. See above, p. 28.

7

RP Today: Its Position and Prospects

Contribution to *Language and Civilisation*, Ed. Alfred Bammesberger and Teresa Kirschner. Festschrift for Professor Otto Hietsch, Regensberg, Peter Lang Publishers, Berne, Frankfort and New York, 1991.

It is about thirty-five years since I last published anything on RP. The reason for this long gap in talking about such an interesting and controversial subject is that I have been away from England, except for occasional visits, during the whole of that time. Of course, there are many opportunities of hearing English people talk on the radio and on television, and I have been teaching at a university – Edinburgh – which attracts many English students. So I am able to say something about phonetic and phonological trends in present-day RP. My chief interest in the accent, though, has always been sociolinguistic, and it is more difficult to discover what is happening in the field from outside England. But let us first look at the phonetic/phonological aspects.

Naturally I do not believe RP has been *phonetically* stable since Daniel Jones described it sixty-five years ago; no-one would expect it to be. No accent or dialect remains static; linguistic change is always at work. I am sure, moreover, that RP has never been as homogeneous as Daniel Jones made it appear. It has always been subject to variations which are personal and idiosyncratic, and this apparently to a much greater extent than other accents of England. RP is therefore difficult, if not impossible, to define phonetically (though there is one feature always present – the extensive use of 'creaky voice'). In other words, it is not phoneticians who say who is an RP speaker and who is not; it is *socially* defined. My own definition (which some find irritating) of an RP speaker is 'someone who is recognised to be so by other RP speakers'.

It is difficult to find any phonetic variations becoming predominant. One may venture to suggest, however, some phonological trends which it seems may prevail. Most conspicuous of these, though it is not very common, is the replacement of the diphthong in, for example, *mouse* by the diphthong in, for example, *mice*. I have seen an RP-speaking character in a comic strip in a newspaper represented as saying 'ight of the hice' for 'out of the house'. This falling together of the two diphthongs does not seem to be known in any other accent of England. I know of only one regular broadcaster who does this, but it may be heard in the speech of certain members of the Royal Family. Other prevalent phonological developments are: the almost universality of 'intrusive' *rs*, as in *idea-r-of, law-r-and order*, though it is as much reprobated as ever; the disappearance of [uə] and its replacement by [ɔ:], as in *poor, sure, during*; and the replacement of [ou] by [ɜ] in many words, for example in *goal*. I have heard *floating* and *flirting* confused. All of these have been present in the speech of some RP speakers for many years.

These observations are based largely on listening to speech on radio and television. Radio broadcasts, and much of television, are put out by the BBC, and at this point a digression on RP and the BBC might be in order. It has popularly been supposed that the BBC used to demand of its announcers that they speak RP, whose use the BBC promoted. 'BBC English' has often been used as a synonym for RP. All BBC announcers did speak RP, it is true, but in fact that was an accidental by-product of another policy: that BBC employees – administrators as well as announcers – should be of good social position, with appropriate interests and tastes. The BBC had an official whose business it was, by interview, to ensure this (he was a high-ranking ex-naval officer). The question of accent never arose; all suitable applicants naturally spoke RP. It is interesting, by the way, that Sir John, later Lord, Reith, the head of the BBC, did not speak RP (he was a Scot). There was an Advisory Committee on Spoken English to the BBC; not all of its members were RP speakers. So it is difficult to make a case for the BBC deliberately promoting RP.

With this digression we can leave the phonetic–phonological aspects of RP, and turn to the sociolinguistic field.

Sociolinguistically speaking, RP is a very remarkable accent. It seems, in fact, to be unique; I do not know of any accent like it anywhere else in the world. There are, of course, accents of great prestige in many countries. These are all regional accents, however; whereas RP is non-regional. It extends over the whole of England, although only a minority of educated people speak it. But it gives this minority privilege and power in many walks of life.

How does such a non-regional accent come to exist? An accent-community is normally geographically based. What can a non-regional accent be based on?

Just as RP is a unique accent, a unique institution provides its basis. This institution is the English Public School, curiously named because it is anything but public: it is extremely private. There are a number of these schools. They are boarding schools, attended by pupils from thirteen to eighteen or nineteen years of age who, while at school, are isolated from their surroundings, though they meet pupils of other Public Schools when playing against them at various sports. These schools are very expensive. RP is never explicitly taught in them, but it is acquired effortlessly from one's fellow pupils, most of whom will anyway already have learnt RP from their families at home.

If children come from a non-RP-speaking family but their parents can afford the expense, and consider it worth it, these children will still join the RP-speaking community, even though their parents remain outside it.

The converse, incidentally, is also true. Some parents who are RP speakers may prefer, for various reasons, not to send their children to a Public School; the children nevertheless will speak RP, and so will belong to the accent community.

From this brief survey of the sociolinguistic background of RP, the crucial fact about it cannot fail to emerge: it is a blatantly undemocratic institution. It is the status symbol of an elite, an aristocracy neither of merit nor of birth, but one whose power is fortuitously arrived at. People are evaluated, not according to their achievements and abilities, but according to their accent.

I have elsewhere claimed that in fact there is in England an 'accent bar', on one side of which are the RP speakers and on the other side the non-RP speakers. I coined the term on the model of the 'colour bar' which is, or has been, found in some societies, and to which an accent bar is in many ways analogous (though of course a colour bar is a much more serious matter). One respect in which they are different is that a colour bar usually has the majority of people on the 'right' side of the bar, whereas the accent bar has only a small minority on the 'right' side.

The consequences of the accent bar can be very varied. For example, the poet Tony Harrison recounts how, when he was a schoolboy (not at a Public School), he was jeered at in class by his English teacher for reading poetry aloud in a local accent instead of in RP. Yet nowadays, with an unchanged local accent, he is considered to be an admirable radio broadcaster of his own poems. In one of his poems he writes 'RIP RP', which aptly sums up the outcome of the accent bar as far as he is concerned (and incidentally shows how the term 'RP' has spread in recent times).

I read in the press recently of a judge's decision concerning the future of a young girl, which provides another example. As the consequence of a divorce, the girl had gone to live with her father, while her brother and sister lived with the mother. The father sent the girl to an expensive school, the result being that she became an RP speaker. Her brother and sister continued to speak with their local accents. The judge, asked to decide on the girl's future, said he accepted that the girl now spoke 'posh' and had moved into a different social class. ('Speaking "posh"' is a popular expression for speaking RP.) She should therefore stay with her father so as not to have to mix with speakers of a socially inferior accent. The accent bar thus ran through the middle of a family.

RP is a much disliked accent in many parts of the world, particularly in Scotland and America. I am an RP speaker, so I speak from experience. It is disliked, as well as envied, by many people in England also. This dislike is becoming more common, and also more outspoken. There are signs that RP's prestige, privileges, and power are being eroded. One ought really to live in England to observe in detail changes which may be taking place, and I do not do so, as I have said; I live in Scotland. Still, much can be gleaned from television and the radio, on which many regular speakers – news readers, presenters, commentators, foreign correspondents, meteorologists – do not nowadays speak RP. In addition to local accents of England, many Scots and Irish accents can also be heard. A large number nowadays are women, moreover. So the public have become quite used to the absence of what used to be thought a necessity for an authority: a male, RP-speaking, voice.

The authority of prominent people in public life, such as Prime Ministers, has traditionally been associated with RP. Prime Ministers this century, whatever their political party, unless they are not English (Lloyd George was Welsh and Ramsay MacDonald was Scottish), have until recently always been RP speakers. We have just seen, however, three successive Prime Ministers who spoke with English regional accents: Harold Wilson, James Callaghan, and Edward Heath. We have now an RP-speaking Prime Minister again in Mrs Thatcher, but if her successor were not, it would occasion no surprise. The tradition has been broken.

Perhaps the most interesting developments are that some speakers of RP seem themselves to be turning against it; and that some young people have elected to speak with a local accent, even though their parents are RP speakers.

Signs of these developments are perceptible even to someone, like myself, living outside England. I have had, for example, at the University of Edinburgh, students from England whose background would lead one to expect them to be RP speakers, but who seem to be deliberately trying to modify their accent by adopting features of other accents, Scots for instance.

I am visited quite often by a number of young relatives of mine – two different families – who were brought up in London by parents one of whom was an RP speaker and whom in the past children would almost certainly have chosen to copy. In both families they have chosen to adopt a local London accent instead. Doubtless the choice was not consciously made; but it seems to reflect a prevailing climate of opinion.

One would really need to be on the spot to assess accurately how general these trends are. It would appear that not much hope can be expected from phoneticians, who seem not very concerned about possible changes in public attitudes to RP and its speakers. Many phoneticians nowadays, moreover, including the most productive and original, are themselves not RP speakers, which may be why they seem indifferent to problems which do not concern them personally.

There are an enormous number of people, all over the world, being taught English, and teaching requires a *pronunciation model* for the learner to emulate. English offers a wide choice of accents suitable as models, more perhaps than most other languages. One of these accents, of course, is RP. It is a very natural, not to say inevitable, choice of model for learners in Europe, and perhaps further afield. Its reputation as a prestige accent is widespread among educators, even if its ambiguous position is not fully realised. The teacher, moreover, has available a large number of pedagogical aids to its use, such as pronouncing dictionaries, disk and tape illustrative recordings, phonetic texts, treatments of special aspects such as intonation, and so on.

Nevertheless, RP has disadvantages as a model. It has a larger vowel system, with many diphthongs, than most accents of English; this can be a teaching problem. It has great prestige in some places, but it arouses hostility or dislike in others. In some parts of the English-speaking world it is not found very intelligible. These points have to be set against its advantages as a model.

RP is probably one of the most widely used models in the English-teaching world, the other being what is usually known as General American, which is really the accent of the Middle West. Although many Europeans mix more with Americans than with British, no one has advocated General American as a model for Europe; indeed there is a widespread feeling that there is something undesirable about an American accent, which is a very old-fashioned attitude. In fact it is a very good model.

Another possible model would be a Scottish accent. It is admired everywhere, is highly intelligible, and phonetically offers a minimum of problems. If provided with pedagogical aids, it would provide an excellent model. But that is another story.

Another possible model would be based on the learners' own mother tongue. Such a model has already appeared in India, Egypt, and West Africa, as I have seen for myself. The advocacy of such a model has been called by an American writer 'the British heresy'. A French expert on language teaching has recently put forward such a model for French learners of English, and presumably this would apply to other European languages. But that, too, is another story.

The position and prospects of RP today, then, it seems to me are not very bright. If I may venture a prophecy, RP is slowly but surely on its way out.

8

The Accents of Standard English in Scotland

Paper given on 15 November 1975 at a conference in the University of Glasgow on 'English as we Speak it in Scotland'. Circulated privately in *Work in Progress* No 10, 1977; and in *The Languages of Scotland*, Eds. A. J. Aitken and T. McArthur, Chambers, Edinburgh 1979.

Although this Conference is called 'English as we Speak it in Scotland', I am afraid that I cannot include myself in that 'we' – as I am sure you are already able to hear. What I have to say is not based on analysis of my own speech, which originates in England. It is based on observations of the students in phonetics I have had in Edinburgh over the past twenty-eight years; or perhaps I should say, rather, it is based on what I have been able to learn from my students' own (supervised) *self*-observation. I will try to give what I have been able to learn with as little use of technicalities as I can.

I want to look at what it is that characterises the way Standard English is pronounced in Scotland, as compared with the rest of the English-speaking world; and I want also to look at what variation in pronunciation exists within Scottish Standard English itself. I shall confine myself to the speech of the Lowlands, mainly because I do not know enough about Highland accents to say much that is useful about them. And I shall not, of course, be concerned with Scots properly so-called, as distinct from Standard English.

All accents, of all languages, have characteristic features of *intonation*, of *rhythm*, and of *voice quality*. These features are the least investigated aspects of Scottish Standard English, and there is not very much of importance in the present state of our knowledge to be said about them. I shall leave these features to the end. It is the so-called *segmental* features that I shall spend most time on: the vowels and consonants of Scottish Standard English, that is to say.

There are four respects in which the segmental features of related accents of a language can differ from each other. I will list them first, and then go on to discuss each in turn. We can have, between accents,

(i) *structural* differences;
(ii) *systemic* differences;
(iii) *distribution* differences; and
(iv) differences of *phonetic realisation*.

Structural differences between accents concern the freedom which specific phonemes have to combine with other phonemes to form structures, such as syllables or words, and more especially with the various restrictions, limitations or constraints which may exist on their freedom to combine or to occur in various places in structures.

Standard English in general, like most languages, has many restrictions on the freedom of segments to combine with each other. There is on sale in Edinburgh a kind of continental quilt called a 'fnug'. This as a trade name is curious, because it contravenes one of the structural restrictions of English, to the effect that a word cannot start with /fn/. (The restriction can be stated in more general terms.) Trade names, new slang words and other coinages, and words borrowed from other languages are usually made to conform strictly with the English structural constraints; in fact combinations of sounds that do not comply are normally found difficult to pronounce by native speakers, and one wonders if 'fnug' will prove a successful name for this kind of quilt. Scots shares, on the whole, most of the structural constraints of the English-speaking world.

However, there is one structural aspect of English which is very important for our present purposes. All the accents of Standard English in the world fall into two classes, depending on whether they are subject to a certain structural restriction or not. This is a restriction on the occurrence of the phoneme /r/ (irrespective of how it may be pronounced; it has, of course, a wide variety of phonetic realisations in the English-speaking world), and is to the effect that /r/ can occur only before a vowel, and not before a consonant or before a pause. Some accents of Standard English are subject to this restriction and some are not. In the accents which are not subject to it, an /r/ can occur just as well before a consonant or a pause as before a vowel; it is a consonant just like any other consonant. These latter accents may be called *rhotic*, to use a convenient technical term which we owe to Dr J. C. Wells of University College, London. The other accents, then, are *non-rhotic*.

My own speech is non-rhotic. All Scottish Standard English accents, on the other hand, are rhotic. Accents of England are divided, very roughly, into those of the west, which are rhotic, and those of the east, which are non-rhotic (though rhotic *dialects*, as distinct from accents of Standard English, can be found in the north-east, around Durham, and in the south-east, in Kent). Irish accents are rhotic. The whole of the middle-west and west of the USA is rhotic, though the east and the south are non-rhotic, for the most part. Most Canadian accents are rhotic; Australian and South African accents are non-rhotic. It is probably true to say that the majority of Standard English speakers in Britain are non-rhotic; and that the majority of Standard English speakers in the English-speaking world are rhotic. From this structural aspect, therefore, Scottish Standard English is a little unusual in Britain, but usual in the English-speaking world as a whole.

Systemic differences concern the number of different vowels and consonants that accents make use of for distinguishing meanings. We need to consider separately the system of consonants and the system of vowels; and it is often convenient, when comparing accents, to consider subsystems of various kinds. For instance, it might be enlightening in some cases to separate a subsystem of word-initial consonants from a subsystem of word-final consonants, or a subsystem of vowels in stressed syllables from a subsystem of vowels in unstressed syllables; and so on.

It is to systemic differences that I want to devote most of my time. They are not very conspicuous differences to the casual listener but they are the most interesting differences linguistically. Before discussing them, however, I must say a few words about the other two kinds of difference between accents – *distribution* differences and differences of *phonetic realisation*.

Distribution differences have nothing to do with structural or systemic differences. They are more conspicuous; they are also linguistically more superficial. They are called distribution differences because they concern the way phonemes are *distributed* in words. Thus it is possible for there to be two accents which have the same consonant and vowel systems, and which have no structural differences, but which nevertheless have different phonemes in the same words. For example, two accents might have different vowel phonemes in *pat* and in *past*, but one might have *photograph* with the *pat* vowel in the last syllable, while the other has the *past* vowel in the last syllable. This therefore is a distribution difference between the two accents. People notice such differences very readily. There are many distribution difference between Scottish Standard English and most other accents of Standard English, both in vowels and in consonants. We find, for example, *housing, houses* with intervocalic /s/ rather than /z/; *Decem-*

ber with /z/ rather than /s/; *sandwich* with medial /ŋ/ rather than /n/; and so on.

Differences of *phonetic realisation* are also independent of structural or systemic differences. Two people speaking the same language may sound very different from each other and yet have identical consonant and vowel systems, and have no structural differences. They sound different from each other because they have different phonetic realisations for some or all of the items in the systems. Differences of this sort, also, are conspicuous, and although they may not be very important linguistically, they are often of great importance socially – particularly in England, but also in other English-speaking countries. Mr Heath, Mr Wilson, and Mrs Thatcher, for example, have three noticeably different accents; but they differ almost entirely in this matter of the phonetic quality of many of the phonemes in their vowel and consonant systems. Scottish Standard English is in general characterised by a number of differences of phonetic quality from accents of England – from, indeed, accents of the greater part of the English-speaking world. For example, many Scottish speakers have a realisation of /l/ which is not homorganic with /t, d, n/, but is dental rather than alveolar. Very noticeable dental allophones of /t, d/, and perhaps /n/, occur when preceded by /l/, as in *world* compared with *word*, *belt* compared with *bet*.

Let us now go back to systemic differences; and first of all to the consonant system. Consonant systems are really quite surprisingly uniform in accents all over the English-speaking world; in fact it is possible to speak of a 'general English consonant system', which is the same, with the occasional omission or addition of an item, for all Standard English speakers. Scottish Standard English, which otherwise has the general English consonant system, has one of these additions. This is the voiceless velar fricative, /x/. No other accent of Standard English possesses it; Scots is unique in this respect. It is not a very common consonant, but nevertheless one hears it frequently enough. It is found in proper names like *Buchan*, *Strachan*; in loan-words from Gaelic, like *loch*; and, from many speakers, in words like *technical*, *technique*. The rest of the English-speaking world uses /k/ in all these words.

There is a great deal more to be said, from the systemic point of view, about vowels than about consonants. Vowel systems are certainly not uniform over the English-speaking world, and it is hardly possible to speak of a 'general English vowel system'. It is in this area that some of the most interesting things about Scottish Standard English are found. In England accents of Standard English do not vary a great deal from each other in their vowel systems, but in Scotland there is considerable systemic variation. I would like at this point to refer to Table 1.

	Scotland	England
bead	1 i	1 i
bid	2 ɪ	2 ɪ
bay	3 e	3 eɪ
bed	4 ɛ	4 ɛ
(never	4a ɛ)	
bad	5 a	5 a
balm		6 ɑ
not	8 ɔ	7 ɒ
nought		8 ɔ
no	9 o	9 oω
pull	11 u	10 ω
pool		11 u
bud	12 ʌ	12 ʌ
side	13 ʌi	14 aɪ
sighed	14 ae	
now	15 ʌu	15 aω
boy	16 ɔe	16 ɒɪ

Table 1

In the Table you will see two columns, one headed Scotland and one headed England. I will explain in a moment what is implied by these headings, and why I want to bring England into this, but first I would like to say a word about how to interpret what is laid out in the Table. In the left-hand column there is a series of key-words, separated by ruled lines. These lines may be prolonged into the next column, like the line between *bead* and *bid*, or they may not, like the line between *bad* and *balm*. The absence of a line means the absence of a distinction between the vowels of the adjacent key-words in the accent that the column represents; but if a line is present, then there is a distinction, and therefore two separate phonemes are involved, not just one. Thus in the Scotland column it is clear that *bad* and *balm* contain the same vowel phoneme; but if one goes across to the England column the ruled line starts again, indicating that in that accent different vowel phonemes are used. So in this way the contrasts between the two systems can be seen at a glance. The number of 'boxes' in a column is the number of different items or phonemes in that system.

In Table 1 the phonemes are identified both by numbers and by symbols. The symbols are not of any great importance; they are convenient, and they are the ones our Scottish students use when transcribing their own speech; but it would be possible to work out other systems of transcription which are just as good. The numbers provide a very convenient way of talking about the phonemes. They are not, of course, numbers for vowel *qualities*, as, for example, Cardinal Vowel numbers are: in other words, they identify the 'boxes', and not their contents.

Let us now compare the two systems which are set out here. I have chosen one accent as representative of Scotland and another one as representative of England – one for Scottish English and one for 'Anglo-English' (a convenient term recently introduced in the correspondence columns of the *Scotsman*). The Anglo-English system is the system of that famous accent called RP, which, as everyone knows, stands for 'Received Pronunciation'; but it is also the system of a number of other, non-RP, accents to be found both in the south and the north of England, and both from rhotic and non-rhotic speakers. It is the most general and the most commonly used vowel system for Standard English in England, though there are, as a matter of fact, a few systemic differences to be found between accents there.

The Scottish system is also a common one, perhaps the commonest among Standard English speakers in Scotland (though I have not been able to verify this), but nevertheless it is only one of a number of Scottish English vowel systems, all of them fairly common. I have named this system the 'Basic Scottish Vowel System'. (I ought to say, to prevent misunderstandings, that the 'immediate constituents' of that phrase are 'Basic' and 'Scottish Vowel System'; they are *not* 'Basic Scottish' and 'Vowel System'. Some people have taken them to be the latter, but what is meant is 'the Basic Vowel System of Scots' and not 'the Vowel System of Basic Scots'. It is necessary to say this, because although there is no such thing as Basic Scots (which seems a nonsensical expression to me) I nevertheless often hear people using the term, having got it, I am afraid, through misinterpreting that phrase of mine.)

I have called it the Basic Vowel System because the other Scottish vowel systems are best described in terms of departures from it; it provides a *basis* for the description of the other systems. In other words it is *descriptively* basic. I do not know if it could be said to be basic in any other sense, though I think one could perhaps say fairly enough that it is the most *Scottish* of the vowel systems of Standard English in Scotland. It seems to me that more than half of our students use it (though many who come from Edinburgh do not).

May I first draw your attention to the vowel which is numbered 4a. I have put it in brackets because it is a kind of 'floating' vowel – it is not an integral part of any Scottish vowel system. It can, in fact, occur with any of them, which is rather an odd situation. That is why I have numbered it 4a, so that it can be inserted into any system without upsetting the numbering of the items following it. Other examples of words in which it is found, in addition to *never*, are *ever, every, seven, seventy, eleven, heaven, devil* (I think all those v's are probably coincidence), *twenty, next, shepherd, whether, bury,* and others.

This vowel might perhaps fairly be called 'Aitken's Vowel', because as far as I know no-one had noticed it until Mr A. J. Aitken drew my attention to it in, I think, 1949. Before that it seems never to have been mentioned in any discussion of Scottish English. Its phonetic quality may be the reason why it escaped notice for so long. It is a fairly centralised vowel, not a fully front one; in fact it sounds very like the vowel I use when I say *never* – my number 4 vowel is always rather centralised, and sounds markedly different from the fully front, or 'peripheral', vowel used by Scots in, for example, the word *dead*. This phonetic similarity between the Anglo-English 4 and the Scottish English 4a may explain the failure in the past to identify the latter as a separate systemic item.

There are a few minor points to be noted about this vowel. First, it has no equivalent in any Anglo-English system or indeed in any vowel system of the rest of the English-speaking world, as far as I know. Second, it is not to be considered as forming part of the Basic System. It is inserted in the Table for convenience, but I have put it in brackets to show its special status. Third, it seems to have a regional basis; it is found in the west of Scotland, in the Borders, and in Perthshire, for example. I formerly believed it was not to be found in Edinburgh, but Mr Aitken has shown me that I was wrong in this. Its geographical distribution needs further investigation. Fourth, speakers who have vowel 4a in their system show great distribution differences between each other; moreover some speakers use it in only a very few words (which means it can very easily escape detection in those speakers, and an investigator may not notice it even after spending quite a lot of time on such an informant), while others use it in quite a lot of words. And fifth, it appears to occur only in stressed syllables.

The Basic Vowel System, as I said just now, is not the only Scottish system. The other systems are best described as modifications of the Basic System towards the Anglo-English system, which is why the right-hand column of Table 1 is there. These are not random modifications; as we shall see, they form a hierarchy. Although they are almost certainly due to influence from England, they are not modifications made by *individuals* to their own speech in imitation of Anglo-English speakers. These other systems are genuine Scottish systems, properly institutionalised, transmitted from parents to children or learnt by children from contemporaries at school. The actual influence from England may have taken place quite far back in time, perhaps in the eighteenth century. A Scot using a vowel system containing some of these modifications towards the Anglo-English system might never even have met an Englishman. We have therefore a *series* of Scottish Standard English vowel systems, and we shall see that they are related to each other in a rather interesting way.

The first modification to the Basic System introduces a distinction corresponding to the Anglo-English distinction between 5 and 6 (you will notice that the Scottish vowels are so numbered in the table that you can insert these additions without upsetting the numbering). Quite a lot of people have this augmented system containing a 5/6 distinction, particularly in Edinburgh; but curiously enough we find here distribution differences between the Scottish system and the normal Anglo-English system, where the former has 6 but the latter 5. This, I believe, is one of the signs of the antiquity of the Scottish system: one would not expect these distribution differences if the influence from England was more immediate. For example, Anglo-English speakers say *gather*, *salmon* with number 5, whereas Scottish speakers with a 5/6 distinction usually say these words with number 6. The following are some of the other words I have noticed which may have 6 in Scottish English but 5 in Anglo-English: *value, alphabet, parallel, paragraph* (in the first syllable), *Cramond*.

Next, a distinction may be added to the Basic System corresponding to the Anglo-English distinction between 7 and 8 – between *not* and *nought*, that is to say. Here again one finds distribution differences between those Scots who have this distinction and speakers in England. The following words, for example, may be pronounced with number 8 in Scotland but number 7 in England: *lorry, squash, squad, watch, wash, yacht.* The interesting thing about the modification of the Basic System by the introduction of this 7/8 distinction is that it is always accompanied by the presence of the 5/6 distinction. Not everybody who distinguishes 5 and 6 also distinguishes 7 and 8, but the converse is the case: everybody who distinguishes 7 and 8 also distinguishes 5 and 6. The presence of the former distinction implies the presence of the latter. I have not so far found an exception to this.

A third modification to the Basic System is possible, and it is easy to guess what this is: the introduction of a distinction between 10 and 11. This is rather rare, and is inconsistently maintained by some of the speakers who have it. It is always accompanied by a 5/6 distinction and a 7/8 distinction, I have found. Distribution differences from Anglo-English speakers may be found here too: for example, the word *food* may be pronounced with 10 in Scotland, but it usually has 11 in England.

So we have four different Scottish vowel systems; the Basic System; the Basic plus a 5/6 distinction; the Basic plus a 5/6 and also a 7/8 distinction; and the Basic plus these two distinctions and also a 10/11 distinction. These are all modifications away from the Basic System towards the England system; but the curious thing is that they do not make the accents which have these augmented systems *sound* any more English than those that do not. In fact, oddly enough, they tend to have the opposite effect, and make them if anything sound more Scottish, because of the very conspicuous distribution differences that I mentioned – they are much more noticeable, to the ordinary listener's ear, than systemic differences. Thus someone who says *salmon* or *gather* with the (originally Anglo-English) number 6 vowel, sounds strikingly Scottish simply because 6 is not used in those words in England.

There are two other ways in which the Basic System can be augmented. First, any of the four systems can have vowel number 4a added, producing, in effect, a further four systems. This, of course, is not a modification towards Anglo-English. Second, there is one more way in which any of the vowel systems enumerated so far can be modified, and which also is not a modification towards Anglo-English; this concerns vowel *length* and *quantity*.

As far as I know, in all accents of Scottish Standard English vowels are long in final stressed open syllables, such as in *agree*, or *brew*, as indeed they are in all accents of Standard English. Scots is exceptional, however, in that if an inflection such as – *d* of the past tense is added to these words, the final vowel maintains its length, whereas in nearly all other accents of English it is shortened. This means that for most Scots speakers there is a distinction of vowel length between *greed*, with a short vowel, and *agreed*, with a long vowel; and similarly between *brood* (short) and *brewed* (long). In most other accents of English the vowels would be the same length. This, of course, is a well-known fact. It would be misleading to take these differences of vowel length as part of the vowel system. It is not so well known, however, that some Scottish accents carry contrasts of vowel length further; they make them where there is no question of an inflection being added. A fairly widespread example of this is a difference between the two words *creek*, with a short vowel, and *creak*, with a long vowel (the vowel quality being the same in both cases). Other examples which I have found of the same kind of opposition of vowel quantity are:

short vowel	long vowel
leek	leak
choke	joke
made	maid
badge	cadge

The etymological reasons for these differences are not obvious. Other accents of Standard English occasionally make such differences: some Australian accents, for instance, distinguish *badge* and *cadge* by a vowel length difference, though oddly enough it is *cadge* that has the short vowel in this case, and *badge* the long one (see D. Laycock, *Le Maître Phonétique*, 1966, p. 22). And in Northern Ireland, in County Antrim, *spoke* (of a wheel), with a short vowel is distinguished from *spoke* (from *speak*) with a long one (see R. J. Gregg, *Orbis*, vol. 7, 1958, pp. 392-406). Gregg thinks this opposition between long and short may be an innovation; it is more likely to be an importation from Scotland.

These length differences distinguish (monomorphemic) words, and are therefore systemic. Here, therefore, is one more possible modification to the Basic Vowel System, one which can be combined with any of the other modifications. So we get a whole hierarchy of Scottish vowel systems, which can be summarised as follows. (I use B as an abbreviation for Basic System.)

$$
\left.
\begin{array}{ll}
\text{Basic System} & \text{13 items} \\
\text{B} + 5/6 & \text{14 items} \\
\text{B} + 5/6,\ 7/8 & \text{15 items} \\
\text{B} + 5/6,\ 7/8 & \\
\quad 10/11 & \text{16 items}
\end{array}
\right\} + 4a \left. \right\}
\begin{array}{l}
+ \text{quantitative} \\
\quad \text{opposition of vowels}
\end{array}
$$

Table 1 sets out, in the Scotland column, the complete Basic Vowel System, therefore; and the other augmented systems discussed so far can also be fitted into it. What appears in the England column, however, is not a complete vowel system, and no complete Anglo-English system can be fitted into it: all the vowel systems of Anglo-English contain additional items that do not appear there. This can be made clear by means of two further tables setting out two subsystems of vowels, in the same manner as in Table 1.

The first of these, Table 2, gives those items of the Basic Scottish Vowel System which appear in syllables closed by /r/, together with the Anglo-English equivalents of these vowels, though of course, Anglo-English being non-rhotic, no /r/ follows them. (Vowel 4a is placed within brackets here, as it is in Table 1. Those Scots speakers who have the vowel in their system are as likely to use it before /r/ as in any other context. Those who do not have it replace it here, as elsewhere, by 4.)

It can be seen that several members of the Anglo-English vowel system – mostly diphthongs – appear in Table 2 which had not been encountered previously in Table 1, i.e. 17, 18, 19, 20, and 21. (It might be mentioned in passing that many speakers of Anglo-English replace 20 by 8.)

Although there are no new items in the Scotland column, many more *different* items appear there than in the England column – nine (or ten if 4a is included) as against six (or five if 20 falls together with 8). It will be noticed in particular that Scottish English can make four distinctions corresponding to the single Anglo-English item 17. Any modifications which may be made to the Scottish system towards the Anglo-English one are likely, therefore, in this restricted context /Vr/ to be in the direction of reducing rather than increasing the number of items. But before discussing such possible modifications, we must note others here which are consequent on two of the modifications to the Basic System already mentioned when Table 1 was being discussed.

The first is a quite straightforward one: if a distinction is made between 5 and 6, then in this particular context 5 will be replaced in all cases by 6.

	Scotland	England
first	2 ɩ	
word	12 ʌ	17 ɜ
heard	4 ɛ	
(herd	4a ɛ̇)	
here	1 i	18 ɩə
fair	3 e	19 ɛə
hard	5 a	6 ɑ
forty	8 ɔ	20 ɔ
four	9 o	
poor	11 u	21 ꭥə

Table 2

The second is somewhat unexpected: if a distinction is made between 7 and 8, then in this particular context 8 is likely to be replaced by 7 – a move *away* from the Anglo-English system, and one which gives rise to fairly conspicuous distribution differences: the use of 7 in *forty, border, short,* for example, is very noticeable to English ears. The reason for this may be that Scottish speakers who have a 7/8 distinction preserve, at the same time, vowel 9 in, for example, *four, boarder, court*; the use of 7 in the context /Vr/ ensures maximum differentiation. (Vowel 9 in this context may be heard also, in more or less the same words, in the rhotic accents of the west of England).

The other modifications to the Basic Vowel System have no repercussions on this subsystem. There are, however, possible modifications to it which are not consequent on modifications to the Basic System.

The first of these is the replacement of 2 by 12: the two, in this context, fall together. This modification may be heard from speakers with the Basic Vowel System, or with any modification to it. It could, I suppose, be said to be a modification towards the Anglo-English system in so far as it reduces by one the number of distinctions at this point.

The second, a more radical modification, is the complete loss of the distinctions between 2, 12, and 4 (and also 4a, if the speaker has it in his system): they all fall together in a true central vowel, which must be reckoned a further addition to the Scottish system, to be identified as 17

	Scotland	England
china	12 ʌ	22 ə
father	20 ɩ	
pitted		2 ɩ
pitied	3 e	

Table 3

(though it differs from the Anglo-English 17 in being 'r-coloured', or pronounced with accompanying retroflexion). This reduction of the /Vr/ system seems never to be heard from speakers who otherwise use the Basic System; it always accompanies other modifications to the system. It is commonly heard from members of the professional classes in Edinburgh, Glasgow, and other towns, and it appears to be on the increase. It clearly is one more modification toward the England system, even though, because of the 'r-colouring', the speaker must be considered to remain rhotic (in fact rhoticity is maintained through all these modifications).

We have so far been speaking of vowels in stressed syllables. Table 3 sets out typical vowels of unstressed syllables, which may be considered to form another subsystem (though many other vowels besides these are found in unstressed syllables, in both Scottish English and Anglo-English).

As in Table 2, Scotland has more items than England has: three as against two. There are no new items under Scotland, but there is one, number 22, under England, a vowel which completes the full inventory of Anglo-English vowels.

Two possible modifications to this Scottish subsystem of unstressed vowels should be noted. The first of these is a regional one: the replacement, in the north-east of Scotland, of 3 by 1.

The second is the replacement of 2, when followed by /r/, by an 'r-coloured' central vowel which may be identified with 22, adding yet another possible item to a maximum Scottish vowel system. This is a modification which goes with the addition to a vowel system of 17; the one implies the other.

Another possible change in Scottish English vowels which modifies them in the direction of Anglo-English is the use of diphthongs instead of monophthongs for vowels 3 and 9. This is not common, and, of course, such a change does not make any difference of system, but merely to the realisation of items in the system.

There is thus a much wider variety of vowel systems in Standard English in Scotland than in England. One more thing is worth noting: the Basic System, with thirteen items, is a remarkably small system for Standard English; as far as I am aware, it is the smallest vowel system in the English-speaking world.

I will have to deal briefly with the remaining characteristics of Scottish Standard English, including the 'non-segmental' features of intonation, voice quality, and rhythm, on which, as I said at the beginning, much work remains to be done.

Intonation is very varied among Standard English accents in Scotland, almost certainly more varied than in England. There has, however, been relatively little investigation of this variation; in fact people seem to have tended to fight shy of it, for it is certainly a difficult subject. There are probably bigger intonation differences to be found between, for instance, Edinburgh and Glasgow, which are only 50 miles or so apart, than within the whole of England; but there has not been much systematic analysis of these differences.

Rhythm is another feature where accents may differ from each other. All accents of Standard English agree in being spoken with what is known as a *stress-timed* rhythm, which means that the stressed, or salient, syllables tend to recur at roughly equal intervals of time, i.e. to be 'isochronous', as distinct from the *syllable-timed* rhythm of many other languages, where all the syllables are isochronous and recur at roughly equal intervals of time. (Not all *dialects* of English are stress-timed. Syllable-timed types of English are found in the West Indies, for example; and West African Pidgin – if indeed it is a kind of English – is syllable-timed.)

However, although all Standard English accents have a stress-timed rhythm, they are not all the same in their rhythmic details, and there is one characteristic of the rhythm of Scottish speech which, once attention is drawn to it, is very noticeable. It is one which I have not come across in any other accent of Standard English. It concerns syllable *quantity* or length. Let me give an example. When I, as one type of speaker from England, say a two-syllable world such as *table*, I give roughly equal length to each of the two syllables. A Yorkshire speaker, on the other hand, will say the word with a long first syllable and a short second syllable; so will a Cockney speaker. Most accents of Standard English have either this equal-equal or this long-short relationship between the two syllables. In Scotland, however, one finds a relationship between the two syllable-lengths which is unusual: the first syllable is short and the second is long. There is, curiously enough, an interesting parallel to this in Scottish music; it is known as the 'Scotch snap', which is typical of Strathspeys and is found in many songs. I cannot help feeling there must be some connection between the occurrence of these two rhythmic facts in those different fields.

Another point might be mentioned while on the subject of syllables. Most accents of Standard English use syllable *division*, on occasion, for distinguishing meanings, making clear the difference between, for example, *a name* and *an aim* by this means. Scots are much less inclined to use such differences for this purpose. In fact, there is much more regularity about syllable division in Scots than elsewhere in English. Scottish speakers make as many syllables *open* syllables as possible (an open syllable is one that ends in a vowel), so that they will attach the final consonant of a word to the beginning of the next word, if it starts with a vowel. Thus they would not distinguish between *a name* and *an aim*: in both cases the *n* would belong to the second syllable. This could be put another way, rather more technically, by saying that in Scots a consonant is made a releasing consonant in a syllable when it is possible to do so. This is uncommon (though not unknown) in other types of English, but it would be the usual thing in some other languages such as French. Thus I constantly hear people say *Sn-tAndrews* for what I would call *Snt-Andrews* (using a hyphen to indicate the syllable division). (We know that *tawdry* comes from *St Audrey*, though this is hardly likely to be due to Scottish influence.)

Voice quality is another aspect of speech which is difficult to investigate and therefore neglected. Scottish accents of Standard English have voice qualities which are characteristic of them, and different from other accents of Standard English; I recognise this when I listen to them, but I find myself unable to say precisely in what the characteristic qualities consist, or even to find adequate descriptive labels for them. The great phonetician Henry Sweet (himself half Scots) claimed that there was a kind of Scottish voice quality familiarly known as 'the pig's whistle'; he attributed the effect to narrowing of the upper glottis or ventricular bands. I have not myself succeeded in identifying the 'pig's whistle' among Scottish speakers, and the expression seems to have fallen into disuse, at any rate in this sense. Some very interesting work on voice quality, however, is being done at the moment in the Department of Linguistics at Edinburgh, which we hope will throw light on the problem of describing and classifying voice qualities in general, and of identifying those which are associated with Scots, and which appear to vary both with region and with social class.

Finally, brief mention might be made of 'weak forms', as they are called: forms of certain words such as prepositions, and pronouns, and others, which come into use when these words are not stressed. They are found in connected speech in all kinds of English. Their occurrence is *syntactically* determined in most Standard English accents: clear rules can be given to describe their use, rules which for the most part do not have exceptions. In Scottish, however, perhaps alone among accents of Standard English, weak forms are *stylistically* rather than syntactically determined: their occurrence depends almost entirely on the speed of talking and on the formality of the occasion. But in any case weak forms are less common in connected speech in Scotland than the rest of the English-speaking world, though at the same time more words have weak forms in Scottish Standard English than elsewhere: *on*, for example, has no weak form in Anglo-English, but it has in Scotland.

Is there anything to be said in general phonetic terms about Scottish Standard English? I think it can, briefly, be characterised as efficient, frugal, and straightforward. It is efficient in being highly intelligible on an international scale. It is frugal systemically: it has a vowel system which does what is needed, with no frills, though it allows itself one small luxury in the consonant system – the voiceless velar fricative – which gives it, perhaps, a touch of distinction. It is straightforward structurally, being rhotic, and does not get involved in such complex matters as linking and intrusive *r*s. It is interesting that it conforms very well to what could be called 'Standard Average European' phonology, many accents of England, particularly RP, being extremely aberrant from European norms.

Because of these things Scottish Standard English provides a very good model of pronunciation for foreign learners of English, particularly since it also escapes the political associations that go with RP and with 'General American', the models that are usually taught.

In conclusion, I would like to say that these remarks on Scottish Standard English are based on the analysis of the accents of about 500 Scottish students at the University of Edinburgh, over the last quarter of a century. I think these students provide a fair sample of Lowland Scottish speakers. For a number of years now nothing very much that is new has cropped up in the way of segmental features. We need, as can be seen, much more investigation of non-segmental features if phonological description of Scottish Standard English is to rank equal with descriptions of what is most unjustifiably widely referred to as 'British English', which is what the English (and Americans!) call RP.

9

Some Functions of Silent Stress

Privately circulated in *Work in Progress* No. 2, 1968. Published in *Edinburgh Studies in English and Scots*, ed. A.J. Aitken, Angus McIntosh, Hermann Pálsson, Longmans, London, 1971.

I am not sure that 'silent stress' is the best term for what I want to discuss here. For one thing, stress is often equated with loudness, so it might at first seem difficult to see how stress could be silent. I prefer, however, to regard stress in a way which has nothing to do with loudness, that is to say as a 'gesture of the respiratory muscles' to use Peter Ladefoged's apt phrase,[1] and a gesture, of course, can be quite silent. For another thing, there are various other terms in this area which might be thought preferable to 'stress' in the present context – 'accent', or 'ictus', for example. Still, the expression 'silent stress' is fairly well established in several quarters, and so I shall continue to use it here, even though I believe it may not be the happiest choice; I believe a careful examination and redefinition of the terminology of this whole area is badly needed. What I want to discuss here is a certain kind of *pause*, found in all kinds of spoken English, which is not, like pauses of other kinds, paralinguistic, but is (potentially, at any rate) phonological – it is part of the structure of an utterance. Let me make clear why I want to call a pause of this kind a 'silent stress'.

English, like most Germanic languages, is a language with (in Pike's terminology) a 'stress-timed' rhythm – in nearly all its forms, at least (some West Indian dialects may have a syllable-timed rhythm, and so may Krio of Sierra Leone). In utterances in a language with stress-timed rhythm, the stresses tend to recur at approximately equal intervals of time; they are isochronous, provided nothing extra-linguistic occurs to prevent this (such as forgetting what one is going to say next). A strong rhythmic beat is thus established, for both the speaker and those listening to him. (It may be observed that the timing of this beat is quite often preserved between participants in conversation, when one speaker takes over from another. This may be especially marked when the conversation is animated. And D.S. MacColl has pointed out that 'any one who studies stage-dialogue will become aware that much of the art of a finished actor depends on *keeping time*, taking up his cue on the right beat'.[2])

However, there is sometimes a pause where a beat, according to the timing already established, might be expected to come, a pause which fills a gap which otherwise would be filled by a stressed syllable. The 'respiratory gesture' of stress, though without accompanying articulatory movements, perhaps still takes place during the pause. I believe it often does do so, even if in an inhibited form. But whether it does so or not is of little importance for our present purposes; the point is that this sort of pause does not throw out the rhythmic beat of stress-timing. It is such a pause, coinciding with the beat, that I call a silent stress. A pause like this is different in kind from other speech pauses. A silent stress is not felt by the listener to be a discontinuity in the utterance; it does not interrupt it, but is part of it; no hesitation is involved.

Not everyone, by any means, believes or has believed in the theory (which goes back to Joshua Steele in the eighteenth century) that English is a language of stress-timed rhythm. A.J. Ellis, for instance, did not believe it, and neither did Henry Sweet. But those who do not believe the theory, it should be noted, do not take account of silent stresses. If one looks for isochronism between stressed *syllables* only, it is fairly certain that, in a stretch of speech of any length, one will not find it. It is the *silent* stresses that keep the isochronous stress-pulse going, in all but the shortest utterances.

The importance of silent stress in the analysis of verse structure has been pointed out by many writers (who have used a variety of names for it), but the existence of silent stresses in other kinds of spoken English has much less frequently been noticed. A few people have drawn attention to them (including Joshua Steele himself), but there has been little systematic attempt to explain why or when they occur, and what sort of functions they perform. An analogy with punctuation, in the written language, has sometimes been drawn, but this does not go very far in explaining their occurrence. I want here to take a preliminary look at some of the functions of silent stress. It seems clear that it has several functions, and that these functions are not equally common in the various modes of use of spoken English. It seems also that sometimes a speaker has a choice whether to insert a silent stress into an utterance or not, so that one may speak of an optional silent stress; and that at other times he *has* to insert one – the silent stress is obligatory. In illustrations of these different functions, I shall use the caret-mark, $\wedge$, to show where a silent stress occurs in an utterance.

One common function of silent stress might be called its *syntactic* function; syntactic silent stresses are closely related to, indeed are part of, the syntax of the utterance. They are found in all kinds of spoken English. Their function can best be demonstrated by comparing sentences which form minimal pairs, and which, in writing and without context, would be ambiguous. A good example is provided by J.P. Thorne in his 'English imperative sentences'.[3] The words 'boys stop here', he points out, can have either an imperative or a declarative interpretation. There are two possible ways of saying the words:

> boys stop here
>
> boys $\wedge$ stop here

In the second of these, Thorne says, the silent stress, coming immediately after the noun, 'removes the possibility of the sentence being taken as a declarative'; it must be an imperative. The ambiguity of the well-known notice 'Gentlemen lift the seat' could be resolved, if spoken, in the same way. Such ambiguities can also be resolved, as Thorne points out, in writing too: 'boys, stop here', with the comma, must be imperative; though perhaps it is sometimes more effective, as in the second example, to refrain in writing from resolving the ambiguity (the sentence is seldom likely to be spoken).

In Act II Scene ii of *Macbeth* we find, after the line 'The multitudinous seas incarnadine', the ambiguous (in writing) phrase 'Making the green one red'. What is the meaning of 'one' here? Is it what Jespersen has called the prop-word, so that 'the green one' means the sea? Or does it go with 'red', so that the meaning is 'a single uniform red'? But it is only in writing that the phrase is ambiguous; in speaking it cannot be. One of the interpretations – the second – requires a silent stress, while the other does not:

> making the green one red
>
> making the green $\wedge$ one red

The different pronunciations are obligatory for the different interpretations. Garrick, it appears, originally used the first interpretation, but later on came to prefer the other one. (In this instance also it is, of course, possible to disambiguate the phrase, by means of a comma, in writing. Some editions have 'Making the green one, red', and others have 'Making the green, one red'. There is also another way of doing it: 'Making the green-one red' and 'Making the green – one red' can also be found.)

Some phrases and sentences may be ambiguous in spoken form as well as in writing, but may still have the possibility of disambiguation by silent stress if necessary. 'Players please' is a rather doubtful example.

Players ∧ please

would seem to be the usual way of giving an order in a tobacconist's shop; but even without the silent stress, the intonation would almost certainly show that a somewhat gratuitous assertion was not being made. But an ambiguous spoken phrase such as 'old men and women' cannot be clarified by intonation only. The two pronunciations

old ∧ men and women

and

old men ∧ and women,

however, will always clear up the ambiguity when it is necessary to do so. The silent stress, in either case, is optional.

Syntactic silent stresses can be heard very frequently in prose read aloud, and they are often obligatory there. The syntax of Dr Johnson's sentence 'Prudence, as it is always wanted, is without great difficulty obtained', for example, demands, when spoken, silent stresses after 'Prudence' and after 'wanted', just as the commas are obligatory in writing. There has been a close connection, at least since the eighteenth century, between punctuation and silent stresses, and it can be observed that most people, when reading aloud, follow a rather rough-and-ready rule that a comma should be given a spoken value of a single silent stress, and the stronger stops two consecutive silent stresses.[4]

Syntactic silent stresses, we have seen, are sometimes optional, sometimes obligatory. J. P. Thorne says, rather cautiously, that 'boys stop here', in its imperative interpretation, *may* be marked by a silent stress. It seems to me, though, that it *must* be; I feel the silent stress to be obligatory for the imperative. I am not sure, on the other hand, that in all contexts this silent stress rules out taking the sentence as a declarative one, as Thorne claims it does. I believe there are occasions when

boys ∧ stop here

could be declarative; but this leads us to recognise that there are other functions of silent stress beside the syntactic. One of these functions might be called *emphatic*: in this function, a silent stress 'points up', gives special prominence to, the word or phrase which follows it. Thus an 'emphatic' silent stress could occur in a declarative sentence in some such context as:

(girls do what they like but) boys ∧ stop here.

This emphatic function of silent stress is a favourite device of radio and television commentators and announcers, but it is common enough in conversation too, as careful listening will reveal. For instance:

The most ∧ awful thing has happened

Another function of silent stress to which I want to draw attention is a curious one. I have not found it in conversation, but it is nevertheless quite common in certain other uses of spoken English, particularly on radio or television. This function is not related to the syntax of the sentence, nor to any of the individual words in it. The silent stress always comes between the last two stressed syllables of the utterance, whatever they are, and usually immediately following the word containing the penultimate stress; and what it does is to signal an immediately impending transition, either from one speaker to another, or from one topic to another. Thus, in the television announcement

The time is nine and a half minutes ∧ to nine

the silent stress is a sign that a continuity announcer has come to the end of what he has to say, and a newsreader is about to take over. We might call this the *terminal* function of silent stress. Such silent stresses are commonly heard in many routine announcements:

BBC Television ∧ from Scotland

but they are often heard in other circumstances as well, as for instance when the title of the record which ends a programme is given thus:

The Way You Look ∧ Tonight

Out of context, utterances containing silent stresses thus placed would seem bizarre and inexplicable. In context, they can often be a valuable guide to the listener, as, for example, in the reading of long lists of football results:

Hearts two Rangers ∧ three

Arsenal one Sheffield United ∧ one

the optional syntactic silent stress after the score of the first team being avoided. This use of terminal silent stress is adopted by many sports commentators.

The terminal function of silent stress may be reinforced by putting more than one in the utterance. I have noticed two, and even three, silent stresses in this function, alternating with the concluding stressed syllables of the utterance. For example, the last sentence of a news item in a television bulletin:

An inquiry into the accident ∧ will open ∧ tomorrow.
The more silent stresses there are, the greater the degree of finality indicated. The following sentence from a television news bulletin was not only the end of the news item, but of the bulletin itself. The story was about a chauffeur and his wife who had just inherited a very large sum from their late employer, and the announcer said:

They wouldn't ∧ be doing anything ∧ extravagant ∧ with the money.

And a similar example from a continuity announcer who was then going off the air:

You'll hear all about it ∧ at ten fifty ∧ in ∧ Grandstand

(the word 'in' receiving a stress). The terminal function of silent stress is not however confined to television and radio. It can be heard, for instance, from many public speakers when they come to the end of what they have to say.

Genuine hesitations in conversation, and other modes of spoken language, are recognised as such by various symptoms, among them being the fact that they tend to throw off the regular beat of the stress-pulse. Hesitations which are not genuine, but feigned in order to give the impression that the speaker is speaking impromptu when he is not, and at that particular moment is seeking for the *mot juste*, are seldom convincing; even when accompanied, as they often are, by a fleeting expression of pain. One reason why they are not convincing is because the speaker usually turns his feigned hesitation into a silent stress and the regular beat is thus not disturbed. (It is indeed very difficult to avoid maintaining the regular beat, and surprisingly often even genuine hesitations are so managed by the speaker that the beat is taken up again at the expected moment. The genuineness of the hesitation must then be revealed by other symptoms.) This – scarcely phonological – function of silent stress could be called *tentative* (more properly, perhaps, *pseudo-tentative*).

The use of silent stresses can easily become, with people who speak a lot in public, an apparently pointless mannerism. Certain television personalities, for example, insert silent stresses into their utterances in quite unpredictable places. The sentence

He has to be all things to all men

would normally be said either without a silent stress, or it could be said with an optional syntactic silent stress after 'things':

He has to be all things ∧ to all men.

However, this sentence was recently spoken by a professional television broadcaster (with the same intonation as one would use in the preceding version) as follows:

He has to be all things to $_\wedge$ all men

where the silent stress seems quite unmotivated (it clearly was not a 'tentative' one, as could be seen from the speaker's air of confidence at that point. Nor was it emphatic, and nobody could be in doubt about what the next words were going to be.) Perhaps this is something comparable to what the Fowlers[5] called 'elegant variation', when talking of writers' choice of words: it is *rhythmic* elegant variation, and does not seem to fulfil any purpose except to be unexpected and different. Perhaps we could call this oddly idiosyncratic, but easily identifiable, use of silent stress its *rhetorical* function.

I have distinguished here, in a rather rough-and-ready way, five functions of silent stress: syntactic, emphatic, terminal, tentative, and rhetorical. Clearly this classification could be refined in various ways, but it may do for a start. It will be of interest to examine, very briefly, how these functions occur in four typically different modes of use of spoken English: conversation, spoken prose, monologue, and verse.

Conversation, as I have pointed out elsewhere,[6] is the least investigated mode of use of spoken English. My rather desultory observations seem to show that, although there is much personal variation, silent stresses in conversation are almost entirely syntactic and emphatic, and that there are relatively not very many of either. In spoken prose silent stresses are very much more common, and they are practically all syntactic.

What appears to be monologue – unscripted uninterrupted talking – is often not, of course: on television the speaker may in fact be reading what he is saying from the teleprompter without the viewer realising it; or someone who is making a speech may have learnt it by heart. But a great deal of genuine monologue exists, in the form of lectures, radio and television commentaries, sermons, and so on, and here one may find all the functions of silent stress, and certainly more of the rhetorical kind than are found elsewhere. (There are many differences, not only in silent stresses, between the way spoken language is used on television and the way it is used on the radio. In the latter, in fact, monologue is rather rare. The differences clearly arise in part from the fact that in the one you can see the speaker, in the other you can not.)

It is in verse that the existence of silent stresses has been most widely recognised, and they have been referred to by various names. For instance, a silent stress within a line is sometimes called a *caesura*, and at the end of a line *catalexis*, or more often *brachycatalexis*, terms which are not very fortunately chosen. *Pause, silent space* and *rest* have also been used, and they at least do not entail confusions with classical prosody. Whatever they may be called, they are almost always syntactic silent stresses, either obligatory or optional. They are, and probably always have been, an integral part of the structure of English verse, as many writers on prosody have admitted. Saintsbury, for example, after saying that a monosyllabic foot 'is always long, strong, stressed, accented, what-not', adds in a footnote 'Except, to speak paradoxically, when it is nothing at all', and he illustrates this (using the caret-mark in the same way as it is used here) by the line from Macbeth i.v:

> Under my battlements. ∧ Come you spirits.

T. S. Omond wrote 'Recognition of these silent spaces is essential to just prosody, and often revolutionises our ideas of a line's structure.' Coventry Patmore, in his 'Essay on Metrical Law', gave an example of how our ideas may be so revolutionised; he pointed out that the line:

> And some I see again sit still, and say but small

is very likely to be read wrong at first sight, without its context, though the rest of the poem makes it clear that an optional syntactic silent stress is required within the line:

> And some I see again ∧ sit still, and say but small.[7]

Silent stresses at the end of the line have a special importance in verse. First of all they serve the purpose of ensuring an even number of beats in the line when the number of stressed syllables, or stressed syllables together with line-internal silent stresses, is uneven, in accordance with the theory that the unit of English verse is the *double* foot. (This, the 'dipode', theory was put forward by Patmore, who called it his 'great general law', and independently by Morris Croll, who did not appear to know Patmore had formulated it first.[8]) Silent stresses at the end of the line also serve as *line-end markers* – they are one of the means by which the line may be delimited as a metrical unit.[9]

Silent stresses may sometimes take a form which is not, strictly speaking, silent: the final sound of the preceding syllable may be prolonged over the space they occupy. This prolongation appears to be in free variation with silence, though it is more common with some people than others. It is, however, curious that emphatic and rhetorical silent stresses seem always to be really silent.

When written language, whether prose or verse, is to be read aloud, there is seldom only one right way of doing it. Obviously, there is almost always a choice in the matter of intonation. There is often also a choice, among other things, in the number and placing of silent stresses. This is of no very great consequence as far as prose is concerned. The choices made are a matter of the reader's taste and experience, and it is often difficult to say why one rendering is more effective than another. In verse, too, such choices must usually be left to taste. Nevertheless, poets must often wish it was not so, though there is not much they can do to ensure that a particular rendering is given to a poem by a reader. Gerard Manley Hopkins clearly felt this strongly, and he used various devices, such as differences in indentation of the lines, acute accents, and various other marks (not always preserved when his poems are printed) in an attempt to ensure the rendering he wanted. Few other poets have made such efforts. There is, however, an interesting problem here. What exactly are the rhythmic constraints introduced by printing words as verse – if any? It seems to be widely believed that the same words, with the same punctuation, are somehow not the same in their rhythmic effect when printed as continuous prose as when printed in lines of verse. Why are they not the same? What difference can the visual arrangement make? There are numbers of examples available. Yeats printed Walter Pater's prose arranged as verse in the *Oxford Book of Modern Verse*; D.S. MacColl printed various passages of prose arranged as verse in *Essays and Studies by Members of the English Association*, v; Saintsbury, in his *Historical Manual*, showed some of Henley's verse printed as prose side-by-side with the original; there is a long correspondence in the *Times Literary Supplement* in the early months of 1965 on the problem in general, and in particular on Hugh MacDiarmid's use of other people's prose in his own poems. It seems possible that the arrangement in lines influences the placing of silent stresses, thereby producing a certain rhythmic effect which is different from the effect produced by a prose arrangement. There are certainly interesting opportunities for speculation here.

NOTES

1. *Three Areas of Experimental Phonetics*, London, 1967 p. v.
2. 'Rhythm in English verse, prose, and speech', *Essays and Studies by members of the English Association*, v, Oxford, 1914, p. 42. n.
3. *Journal of Linguistics*, 2, 1966, pp. 69–78.
4. This, in effect, is the advice given to young preachers in P.E. Sangster,

Speech in the Pulpit, London, 1958, where caret-marks are used in the same way as here. An interesting account of the development of punctuation marks and their connection with what the author calls 'time-pauses' can be found in A. C. Partridge, *Orthography in Shakespeare and Elizabethan Drama,* London, 1964.

5. In *The King's English* and *A Dictionary of Modern English Usage.*
6. *Studies in Phonetics and Linguistics,* London, 1965, Ch. I.
7. See G. Saintsbury, *Historical Manual of English Prosody,* London, 1910, p. 23; T. S. Omond, *English Metrists,* Oxford, 1921, pp. 176; Coventry Patmore, *Poems,* second collective edn, 2, London, 1886, pp. 241.
8. Patmore, *op. cit.* pp. 242; 'The Elementary measure, or integer, of English verse is double the measure of ordinary prose, – that is to say, it is the space which is bounded by *alternate* accents.' See also Morris W. Croll, *The Rhythm of English Verse,* Princeton, NJ, 1925 (mimeographed. This scarce and little-known work is now available in *Style, Rhetoric and Rhythm,* Essays by Morris W. Croll edited by J. Max Patrick *et. al.,* Princeton, NJ, 1966.)
9. See Thomas Taig, *Rhythm and Metre,* Cardiff, 1929, p. 39. I owe to Angus McIntosh my knowledge of this remarkable book.

10

'Stress' and Some Other Terms

Paper given to the National Phonetics Colloquium, Leeds, March 1960

No apology is needed for this attempt to desynonymise and disambiguate this troubled area. I do not, in fact, suggest departing radically from the way many other linguists have used the words. I will start with the word 'stress' itself. Note that I am not saying what stress 'is', but suggesting a way in which the word 'stress' can profitably be used. When I speak of 'definition', 'nominal' and not 'real' definition is intended.

I want, first of all, to suggest that *stress* should be confined strictly to *general phonetic* discussions. There are many general phonetic terms which are traditionally used as phonological terms also. In this particular case I feel strongly that this should be avoided (at least in discussing certain languages: 'voiced' and 'voiceless' in English are other instances). Many pseudo-problems, leading to fruitless arguments, can arise, and have arisen, if care is not taken to confine the term to one level – in this case, the general phonetic one.

I would restrict the word, moreover, to something which is *either present or absent*; that is to say, I would not use it as a scalar or gradient term, i.e. for something which is always present in varying degrees (as, for example, Sweet used the word, and as many others have). Thus, I would avoid, for example, the expression 'secondary stress'. A syllable is either 'stressed' or 'unstressed'.

This something which may be present or not is 'a gesture of the respiratory muscles' to use Peter Ladefoged's expression. In defining it in terms of the pulmonic air-stream I follow a more or less Stetsonian line: I would say that stress is a reinforcement of a breath-pulse, a muscular action which produces a higher sub-glottal air-pressure (of which the speaker is kinesthetically aware, and of which the listener may be aware by 'empathy'). But I think non-Stetsonians can use the term for an *activity of the speaker* without committing themselves to any other part of Stetsonian theory.

I wish to define stress without attaching to the definition any accompanying symptoms or clues by which the listener recognises it when it occurs in speech. The definition is in terms of the airstream mechanism only, and of the action of no other parts of the speech-producing process. Stress as thus defined is not *as such* audible; it can only be kinesthetically perceived. There may be other things which are symptoms of the presence of stress, but I do not make them *part of* stress.

One particularly strong reason for excluding articulatory and auditory symptoms of the presence of stress from my definition of it, is that such clues, with the possible exception of loudness, are apt to be language-specific, and not inevitable consequences of the coincidence of a 'stress-gesture' with a syllable.[1] Such clues are, of course, of the most varied nature. (Loudness is a poor clue to the presence of stress on a syllable anyway, and is probably never the only one. In any case it cannot, at present, be measured satisfactorily.)

Syllables therefore are either stressed or unstressed. It is also possible, with this definition, to speak of 'silent stress', making a useful distinction between 'stress' by itself and 'stressed syllable' – a stress *plus* part of an utterance. (We can say, therefore, that the important thing about English verse is the number of stresses per line, not the number of stressed syllables; some of the stresses may be silent.)

Objective, instrumental, evidence of the occurrence of stress as here defined can probably be provided; but I am prepared to take the speaker's word for it.

What I have put forward here as a definition of stress has formed part of many other people's definition of the term, but I exclude strictly the rest of what has nearly always been included under it.

It is possible that all languages are normally spoken with stress in my sense; and also possible that they can all be spoken intelligibly without the use of stress (provided no other features are changed), if one cares to learn to do so.

I wish to use *accent*, which has often been a synonym of 'stress', in a very different way, in a sense which is not general phonetic at all. This sense has no auditory and no physiological characteristics attached to it whatever. Accent, as I use it, exists only at the lexical level.

When I say that such-and-such a syllable of a word has an (or the) accent, or is accented (other syllables therefore being unaccented), I am not saying anything about the phonetic characteristics of that syllable. All that is being said is that in certain conditions (which must be specified) in utterances, an accented syllable will show certain characteristics which can be predicted, and these may be different from its characteristics in other conditions. The various possible realisations of accent may have nothing phonetic in common. An accented syllable *may* be realised with stress, with various features of pitch, of syllable length and segment length, of loudness, and of articulatory characteristics in various combinations. But none of these are included in the definition of accent. In other words, accent itself is ineffable. It plays no part in the phonological analysis of utterances; its place is in the lexicon. Accent, in fact, is what is indicated by the 'stress marks' in the *English Pronouncing Dictionary*.

While French has *stress*, it does not have *accent*.

'Accent' is more or less the same as what many have called 'word-stress' (though others have used this to refer to the mode of realisation of accent in a citation-utterance of a word). We need another term, beside 'stress' and 'accent', for what has been called 'sentence-stress' (which also has other meanings). We need a word for the property of being the first syllable in a foot, the syllable on which the beat of stress-timing falls. This I have called *salience*, the first syllable in the foot being the 'salient syllable'.

We can now define 'accent' as a *potentiality for salience*. The salient syllables of an utterance will always, in English, coincide with accented syllables, at least in normal spoken English; but of course accented syllables are often not realised as salient ones.

I have not here suggested any use for the words 'prominent' and 'prominence', which Daniel Jones introduced as technical terms in, I think, 1932, in the third edition of the *Outline*. I originally used 'prominence' (with reluctance) instead of 'salience'; but I have come to think it is better eschewed as a technical term altogether, at any rate for the time being – it has been much abused. There is no reason, however, why it should not be used in its ordinary, everyday sense in discussions of these topics. Thus one can say that salient syllables – and other words containing them – are prominent, i.e. particularly noticeable, to the listener; but one need not expect them to be prominent to someone who is not listening to his mother tongue.

I have, however, found a fourth term useful: *ictus*. In considering the foot as a structure, one needs, for the 'places' in structure, names which are distinct from the names of the elements which may fill those places. The foot has two places, and 'ictus' is a convenient name for the first (I have called the second place the *remiss*, to borrow a term from, and so do some small homage to, Joshua Steele). But though I think such a term is necessary, I do not expect it to find any wide use: the phonology of the foot is not widely discussed.

NOTES

1. See, for example, I. Fonagy, *Phonetica*, 2, 1958.

11

The Indication of Pronunciation in Reference Books

Paper given to the Dictionaries Group, European Group of Educational Publishers, at a Conference held at Peebles in June 1977. Published in *In Honour of A. S. Hornby*, ed. P. Strevens, Oxford University Press, London, 1978.

The indication of pronunciation in works of reference is rather more complex than might at first be supposed. A number of dubious decisions of various sorts have been made in the matter in reference books in the past, and it is worth taking a look at eight different areas in which decisions have to be made.

(*1*) The first and the most fundamental decision which must be made by the compilers of a work of reference is whether to give any indications of pronunciation at all. There seems to be a tendency in recent times to include indication of pronunciation even when this does not appear to add to the work's usefulness. One wonders, for example, whether etymological dictionaries have any need to show pronunciation. Skeat's *Etymological Dictionary of the English Language* (1879–82), Weekley's *Etymological Dictionary of Modern English* (1921), and the concise versions of both (1882 and 1924, respectively) give no pronunciations; but the more recent *Oxford Dictionary of English Etymology* (1966) does, though their relevance is difficult to see. Very many reference works in the past had no indications of pronunciation, and in most cases they seem to lose nothing by their absence. There are none in early editions of the *Encyclopaedia Britannica* (and only occasional ones in later editions), in *Chambers Scots Dictionary*, in *Hobson-Jobson*, in the first edition of the *Oxford Dictionary of English Christian Names*, to take a few random examples. I have often wondered whether the big *Oxford English Dictionary* (1888–1928) really needed to show pronunciations; I doubt very much whether anyone ever uses it to verify how a word sounds. I do not think it should be taken for granted that indication of pronunciation is a necessary part of an entry in a work of reference. It seems to me that in contemporary reference books pronunciation is shown more often than it need be.

(2) If indications of pronunciation are to be given, how extensive should they be? Should they be given for certain aspects of pronunciation only? Should they be given for every word, or only for certain words, or only for part of words? The earliest indications of pronunciation in reference books were confined to stress; that is all there is in Dr Johnson's *Dictionary of the English Language* (1755) for example, where it is shown by 'printing an accent upon the acute or elevated syllable'. This is probably still all that is needed for many types of reference book intended for native speakers; it is often needed only for certain words. Thus Onions's *Shakespeare Glossary* (1911) confines indications of stress to words where its incidence is unexpected. All the same, it undoubtedly is necessary, in many types of reference book, to indicate, in addition to stress, the sounds of vowels and sometimes of consonants (it is the vowels that cause most of the trouble in English). Should this be done in every entry? Not necessarily, it seems to me. *The Concise Oxford Dictionary of Current English* (1911) indicated the incidence of stress in all cases, but gave information about vowels and consonants only when the spelling is ambiguous (the sixth edition [1976], however, now gives fairly full phonetic information for almost every headword, even identifying the vowels in *dog* and *cat*, so perhaps exemplifying the recent tendency referred to above). *Longmans English Larousse* (1968) gave a full transcription for each word, though the French original on which it is modelled confines itself to points of possible ambiguity – such as in the word 'guillotine', which is followed in the entry by '(*ghi, ll* mll)', which tells one all one needs to know – if one is French ('mll' meaning *mouillé*). *The Stanford Dictionary of Anglicised Words and Phrases* (1892) indicates the stress patterns of occasional words, and no more.

(3) Should pronunciation be indicated on the headword itself, or should it be given separately? There are various ways of incorporating it in the headword: by placing diacritics over or under letters, for example; or by using different founts of type, such as italic or black-letter, for certain letters; or by putting numbers over letters (usually the vowels). The use of different founts is on the whole a bad expedient, and not much used nowadays; but numbers over vowels have been used very effectively in recent times in works by Michael West, for example, and they were once quite widely used, as in the dictionaries of Kenrick and Sheridan, for instance. Nowadays diacritics, though somewhat unsightly, are the preferred device. The incorporation of

pronunciation in the headword is, of course, a considerable space-saver.

(4) If pronunciation is to be shown separately from the headword, should the method be (a) by a 're-spelling' system; or (b) by phonetic transcription? The former is based essentially on the orthographic conventions of English, often with diacritics added; the latter uses vowel letters with radically different values from the traditional English ones, introduces new letters, and is usually 'bi-unique', i.e. each sound has only one symbol and each symbol has only one sound (re-spelling systems are usually not bi-unique). These are really two extremes, and many possibilities lie between.

Sometimes both methods have been used at the same time, as, for example, in Henry Cecil Wyld's *Universal English Dictionary* (1932), A. Lloyd James's *Broadcast English* (eight parts, 1928–39), or G. M. Miller's *BBC Pronouncing Dictionary of British Names* (1971). The use of both methods simultaneously is, however, expensive of space, and usually a choice must be made between the one and the other.

It is widely believed that the use of phonetic transcription offends native speakers, and that the use of re-spelling is considered unscientific by foreigners. These beliefs are very possibly true; in any case a decision between the two alternatives is normally based on them.

(5) If a re-spelling system is to be used, what type should be chosen? There are many possible varieties. These arise because it is not possible to re-spell completely unambiguously every English word in accordance with traditional orthographic conventions. Some way has to be found, for instance, of indicating the difference in vowel sound between *good* and *food*; of dealing with the unstressed vowels in *about*, *token, flagon, column*; of distinguishing the initial consonants in *think* and *then*; of identifying the medial consonant in *vision*; and so on. A re-spelling system has to be supplemented by other devices, therefore, such as diacritics, italics, digraphs, even new letters.

A simple and straightforward system, needing little explanation, is used by the BBC Pronunciation Unit in the weekly list distributed internally of those proper names which are at the moment in the news. Another good system is that used in *Chambers Twentieth Century Dictionary*; by introducing one new letter, e , it is able to deal neatly with a number of problems. Webster's *Third New International Dictionary* introduces both e and another new letter, n, for the final sound in *hang*; and it also employs the ingenious device of using ? when there is a choice in pronunciation between e and i, as in the final syllable of *private*. Their re-spelling system, in fact, comes very close to being a phonetic transcription.

It is worth pointing out that a re-spelling system, if it is to be effective, needs just as much advice from a phonetician as a phonetic transcription does.

(6) If phonetic transcription is preferred to re-spelling, a decision still has to be made concerning the type of transcription to be used. Many different systems of phonetic transcription are in existence. Wyld's *Universal English Dictionary*, for instance, uses a transcription of his own, which appears in other books of his (it derives ultimately from Henry Sweet). *The Oxford Dictionary of English Etymology* uses a simplified version of the transcription devised by Murray for the *OED*, which itself is probably the most complicated system of indicating pronunciation ever used in a reference book: it contains over fifty symbols for vowels alone.

However, this decision is not a difficult one, for most people nowadays would opt for a transcription using the alphabet and following the principles of the International Phonetic Association (IPA), and most other systems of phonetic notation have fallen into disuse (though the *OED* Supplements stick to the original complex system).

(7) If the decision is made to use an IPA transcription, which of the many varieties which conform to its principles and use its alphabet should be chosen? What is called 'the IPA transcription' by lexicographers is usually just one of these varieties, the one used in Daniel Jones's famous *English Pronouncing Dictionary* (1917). It is often also called 'the Daniel Jones transcription', though he did not invent it, and he did not make much use of it in his other works. It has a number of defects, and Jones made a bad decision when he chose this variety (best referred to as 'EPD transcription', after the initials of the dictionary) – if indeed the decision was his: he possibly inherited the transcription from an earlier pronouncing dictionary which used the same transcription – *A Phonetic Dictionary of the English Language* (1913). Jones produced this under the general editorship of Hermann Michaelis, who very possibly was responsible for the decision. In any case, Jones experimented widely with other varieties of IPA transcription, and some of these are much more suitable for use in reference books; one might mention in particular the type which Jones called 'extra-broad', which has only seven different vowel letters; it is used in P. A. D. MacCarthy's *An English Pronouncing Vocabulary* (1945). This and other varieties of IPA transcription are sometimes referred to

as 'modified IPA' in reference books, when what in fact is meant is 'modified EPD'.

However, the fact is that Jones's *English Pronouncing Dictionary* is the most famous of all pronouncing dictionaries, and the type of transcription it uses has in consequence great prestige. Compilers of reference books are apt to find that customers demand that they too should use it, in spite of its many shortcomings. It has now, in the last (fourteenth) edition, been very considerably modified by Professor A. C. Gimson, who has taken over the editorship; it remains to be seen whether the new type of transcription will attain the prestige of the old one, and whether the expression 'EPD transcription' will take on a new meaning.

(*8*) One last important decision remains: what accent of English ought to be represented? With many languages one would not have to worry about such a question, but it is a very real problem for a reference book in English. Those produced in America, for internal consumption, will, of course, choose an American accent, probably the one rather vaguely called 'General American'; but what should reference books intended for the rest of the world – English-speaking or English-learning – choose? A very large number choose, in fact, the accent of England called 'RP', and customers often demand that this should be the choice. All the same, it is probably not the best accent to choose. It is the accent of a small minority of people, even in England, and it is not really representative of accents of English, being, as it is, 'non-rhotic' (meaning that *r* is pronounced only at the beginning, and not at the end, of syllables).

In the *Twentieth Century Dictionary* the preliminaries explain that the re-spelling system used in it 'allows for more than one interpretation so that each user of the dictionary may choose a pronunciation in keeping with the rest of his speech'. Such a system of indicating pronunciation is clearly a great advantage; but as a matter of fact most types of phonetic transcription also allow of it, at least to a certain extent, and there are 'multi-accent' types of transcription which are deliberately designed to allow it. Here lies, I feel sure, the reason behind the extraordinary complexity of the *OED* transcription (though the preliminaries do not make this entirely explicit). (The *Supplements*, astonishingly, now claim that 'the pronunciations given are those in use in the educated speech of southern England'; if that were really so, there would be no need of fifty different symbols for vowels.) A 'multi-accent' transcription, naturally, is no longer 'bi-unique'. It is worth mentioning, incidentally, that from this point of view the increasingly fashionable use of /əu/, instead of /ou/, for the vowel in *go* is a retrograde step: the former imposes a more limited interpretation than the latter.

It goes without saying that, whatever method of indicating pronunciation is adopted, it should be consistently and correctly used in the body of the work, and that the pronunciations themselves should be plausible. It is disappointing to find how many reference books fall short of these elementary requirements, and how many, moreover, contain misprints in the pronunciations – an area where misprints are probably more damaging than anywhere else. It ought to go without saying also that the method of indicating pronunciation should be adequately explained in the preliminaries, but all too often this is not so, and the explanations fall short of what a reader needs. *The Stanford Dictionary*, for instance, distinguishes three degrees of stress which are duly, though briefly, noted in the Introduction, but one looks in vain for an explanation of why pairs such as *hubbub* and *humour*, *incitement* and *inspector*, *calculator* and *incubator,* should each show two different stress patterns. Sometimes, indeed, no key at all to the pronunciation is to be found in the front-matter. *The Oxford Dictionary of English Christian Names* gives no explanation of the re-spelling system it uses. Perhaps the interpretation of the system was thought to be self-evident. All the same, the attentive reader can hardly fail to be puzzled on finding that the final vowel-sound of *Griselda*, *Pamela*, and *Roberta* has a different symbol to represent it from the one allotted to the final vowel-sound of *Diana*, *Fenella*, and *Tamara*; and that both symbols are different from the one given to the final vowel-sound in *Elfreda*, *Maria*, and *Teresa*. He will also notice that *Dante* and *Ianthe* are re-spelled with different vowel symbols at the end, and may wonder why. The same applies to the final syllables of *Antoinette* and *Bernadette*. It is, of course, possible that all these discrepancies involve misprints. Misprints and inconsistencies in, and omission of symbols from, keys to pronunciation are more serious; but they are regrettably common, even in reference books clearly in other respects carefully edited.

As I said at the beginning, it seems possible that the problems involved in exhibiting pronunciation in reference books are generally underestimated.

12

Phonetic Iconicity in Writing Systems

Paper given, 18 November 1977, at the School of Oriental and African Studies, London.

The shape or form of a letter may be an articulation diagram. It is then an iconic sign, or icon, in the terminology of the American philosopher C. S. Peirce; an icon has some likeness, qualitative or structural, to its object. Such a letterform is 'phonetically iconic', one could say, as distinct from the different kind of iconicity exemplified in Chinese writing, for example.

An articulation diagram, though, is only one possible way of producing a phonetically iconic letterform. There are two other possible types of letterforms which also show phonetic iconicity.

One of these types would be letterforms which refer to *sound*, rather than to the articulatory posture which produces the sound: the iconicity is then *acoustic* rather than physiological. Obviously, this is a difficult thing to bring about, and I know of only one serious attempt to do it: it is illustrated in the book *Visible Speech* (1947), by Potter, Kopp, and Green. In their suggested script the letterforms were derived from simplified sound-spectrograms (see Figure 1). The signs are legible and moderately easy to write. They were devised mainly to help people to learn to read actual sound-spectrograms; but I think the idea is now more or less forgotten.

A third way in which phonetically iconic signs for a writing system can be produced is by what might be called '*taxonomic* iconicity', or maybe 'iconicity by analogy'. In the two preceding types of iconic notation the individual sign is *in itself* iconic, it is a direct representation of a sound or a posture; but in this type the sign is not in itself iconic; it only becomes iconic by being related to a system of phonetic classification: the shapes show similarities to each other which correspond to classificatory or taxonomic similarities. The idea is a simple

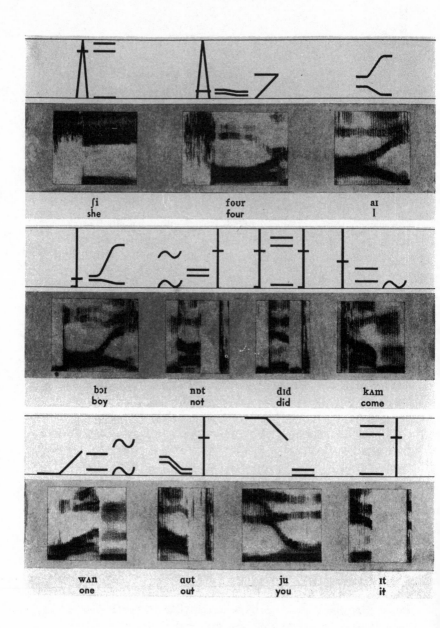

Figure 1

one but somewhat complicated to explain, and it is most easily understood from illustrations. A good one is the system of shorthand
invented by Isaac Pitman in 1837. In this system the signs for consonants are related to the traditional classification by 'place and manner';
thus stops are represented by straight lines, fricatives by curved lines,
labials by backward sloping signs, alveolars and dentals by vertical
signs, velars by horizontal ones. Voiceless sounds are given thin lines,
voiced sounds thick lines. Consequently, a simple sign like ∣, which
taken in isolation is not iconic, becomes so when taken in relation to all
the other signs in the system: we know it must be a stop, which is
alveolar and voiceless. It is in fact a compressed three-term taxonomic
label. Most shorthands invented since Pitman's have been iconic in this
way – even Henry Sweet's system (1892). Pitman, however, was the
first to carry out the idea with such consistency.

But what I want to talk about mainly is the first kind of phonetic
iconicity, the articulatory kind. This has fascinated people for many
centuries. There are two theories involving the idea.

The first theory, the weaker one, holds that writing systems *ought* to
be iconic; while the second, a stronger one, holds that writing systems
are iconic. In other words, this second theory claims that most writing
systems originate with articulatory iconic signs, however much the
passage of time may have disguised their iconicity, while the weaker
theory is to the effect that – whether or not existing writing systems
were in origin iconic – any *new* writing systems should be created on
this basis.

Various people have put forward the stronger theory in the past. Van
Helmont made the claim for Hebrew writing in the seventeenth century. Sir William Jones said, in 1786, 'all the symbols of sound ... at
first, probably, were only rude outlines of the different organs of
speech'.

The other theory also goes back a long way. John Wilkins, for
example, wrote in his *Essay Towards a Real Character* (1668), 'there
should be some kind of sutableness, or correspondency of the figures
to the nature and kind of the Letters which they express' ('letter' here
does not mean, of course, 'written character'). His own 'Natural
Character of the Letters' is well known. He admits it is 'complicate'; in
it the signs have 'some resemblance to that configuration which there
is in the organs of speech upon the framing of several Letters' (see
Figure 2). The signs can be seen in the top right-hand corner of each
square, which is filled mostly by a diagram of the articulatory posture

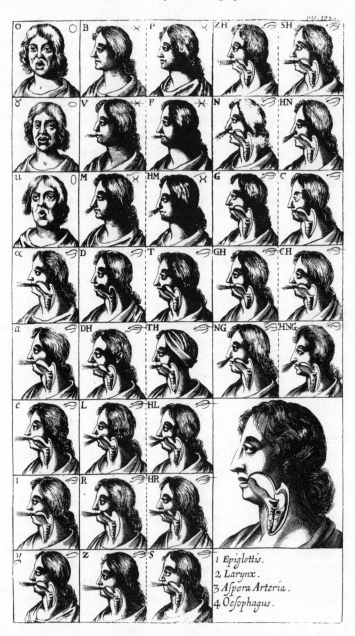

Figure 2

concerned. The signs consist, for the most part, of a line representing the tongue and another representing the roof of the mouth, i.e. 'the chief out-lines representing the organs of speech'.

I do not think that Wilkins meant to do more here than illustrate a principle; certainly this 'Natural Character' would be most laborious to write and very difficult to read, and Wilkins devised two other, much more practical, notations (one of them roman-based).

Other people tried the same thing. Figure 3 shows the frontispiece from van Helmont's book showing someone at work on devising an articulatory iconic notation, and taking careful measurements. But most of these inventors, unlike Wilkins, really did intend their systems for practical use. One of these was the 'Natural Short-hand' published by William Holdsworth and William Aldridge 'of the Bank of England', as they described themselves. It appeared in 1766. In this system, to quote from the title-page, 'every single articulation whether vowel or consonant is marked by a distinct single line. All the simple characters are as analogous to each other as the sounds they represent.' Figure 4 is the plate from the book showing how this was carried out. 'The particular form of every simple character should correspond with the natural position of the organs of speech, or the passage of the breath, in the act of pronunciation.' As articulatory diagrams, the characters are pretty skeletal; but in a shorthand they could hardly be anything else. Even so, I do not think that as a shorthand it was very short. In any case I doubt if many learnt it, and the book had only one edition – in contrast to the enormous success of Byrom's system, published the year after. I do not know of any other shorthands which had an articulatory iconic basis.

There have, however, been plenty of general phonetic notations with an articulatorily iconic basis. Much the most famous of these is the one invented by Alexander Melville Bell, which he called 'Visible Speech' made public in the book of that name in 1867 (Potter, Kopp, and Green borrowed the title for their own book in 1947).

Visible Speech was to inaugurate 'a new science of Universal Alphabetics'. Bell really did think that 'the idea of representing the mechanism of speech-sounds in their alphabetical symbols' was new. It was not, of course. Still, it was undoubtedly the most carefully worked out iconic notation so far. It had an astonishing success. It was learnt – from Bell himself – by James Murray, the editor of the *OED*; he wanted to make use of it in the Dictionary, but Oxford University Press would not allow it. Alexander Graham Bell, the inventor's son,

Figure 3

III

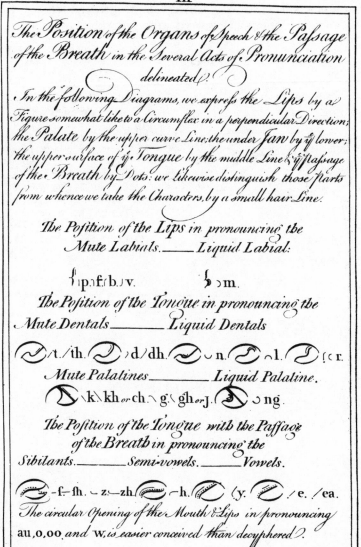

Figure 4

DIAGRAMS SHOWING THE RELATION OF THE PRIMARY
ORGANIC SYMBOLS TO THE ORGANS.

CONSONANTS.

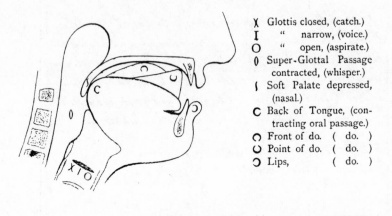

Ӿ Glottis closed, (catch.)
I   "   narrow, (voice.)
O   "   open, (aspirate.)
0 Super-Glottal Passage
   contracted, (whisper.)
ʃ Soft Palate depressed,
   (nasal.)
C Back of Tongue, (con-
   tracting oral passage.)
ꞓ Front of do. (do.)
ꞟ Point of do. (do.)
ꞓ Lips,   (do.)

VOWELS.

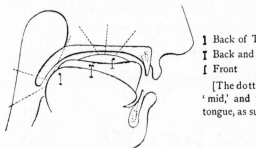

1 Back of Tongue high.
ᵼ Back and Front do. do.
ʃ Front   do. do.

[The dotted lines show the 'high,
'mid,' and 'low' positions of the
tongue, as subsequently explained.]

Figure 5

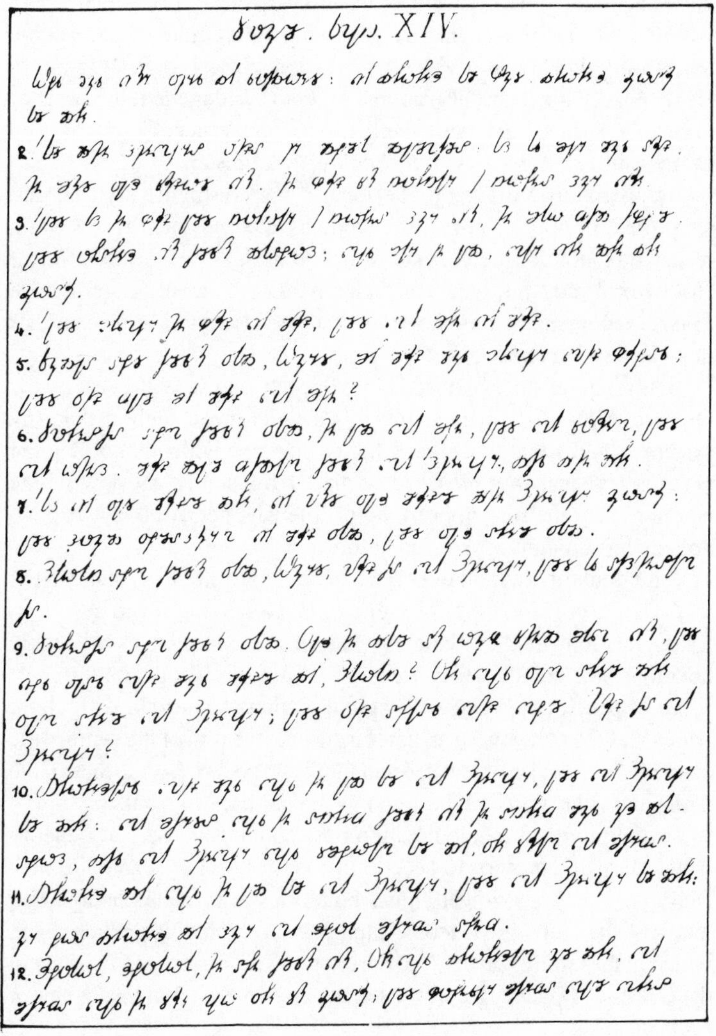

Figure 6

learnt it as a child and used it all his life, particularly in his work with the deaf; and many others used it for teaching the deaf also. A plate from *Visible Speech* is given in Figure 5 showing the articulatory basis of the letterforms. There was also a script version of the system (Figure 6). Henry Sweet also learnt it from the inventor, and made it the basis of his own 'Organic Alphabet' which also had great success – it was used for texts in *The American Anthropologist*, for instance.

As articulatory diagrams the letterforms are highly stylised and simplified, of course; in fact the iconicity of the system is at several places taxonomic rather than articulatory. This is true also of Holdsworth and Aldridge; in fact, all articulatorily iconic systems have to have recourse, at some point or other, to taxonomically iconic, or quite arbitrary, elements in their signs.

Bell set great store by his Visible Speech, and so did Sweet by his Organic Alpahabet. In fact, there is a widespread feeling that any system of signs that is iconic is better than one which is not. People perhaps feel that it is closer to reality. I frequently get new iconic notations sent me for criticism, by people who nearly always believe nobody has thought of the idea before.

But I doubt if we shall ever see a better iconic notation than Bell's; and alas as a notation it was not very good, even as improved by Sweet. It has inherent defects which I suspect are common to all iconic notations. For example, they are liable to quite accidental misfortunes: Visible Speech was based on a sagittal section of a head looking right, which was the convention at that time. But at the turn of the century the conventional head got reversed and looked the other way, so that all the labial and velar signs (and others) were then back to front.

Furthermore, an iconic notation may commit its users to a theory which they do not wish to accept: this is the case, for example, with Bell's and Sweet's vowel signs. Finally, it seems inescapable that many of the signs in an iconic alphabet look much too much alike, which makes things difficult for printer and proofreader. Misprints in the Organic Alphabet got past even the careful Sweet in his *Primer of Phonetics*.

An iconic basis for a notation probably has mnemonic value, and it simplifies the learning of modern iconic shorthands. But iconic notations of any sort, once they have been properly learnt, work, as far as reading and writing are concerned, like any other notations.

13

Paralanguage

British Journal of Disorders of Communication vol. 3, pp. 55-59, 1968.
Published in *Readings for Applied Linguistics*, ed. J. P. E. Allen and S. Pit
Corder, Oxford University Press, London, 1973, under the title
'Paralinguistic Communication'.

We speak with our vocal organs, but we converse with our entire
bodies; conversation consists of much more than a simple interchange
of spoken words. The term *paralanguage* is increasingly commonly
used to refer to non-verbal communicating activities which accompany
verbal behaviour in conversation. Anyone with a professional interest
in spoken language is likely, sooner or later, to have to take an interest
in paralanguage too.

I do not, all the same, like the term paralanguage very much,
although I have used it for my title, and although it has been widely
adopted. It seems to me potentially misleading: it can give the impression that, because there exists a (more or less) homogeneous entity
called *language*, there must be, existing beside it, a comparably homogeneous entity called *paralanguage*. I believe this is not so. (The word
paralinguistics, I regret to say, has already emerged as a name for a
new subject, the study of paralanguage; and we may be sure that
paralinguist, or *paralinguistician* will not be far behind to designate
the person who practises it.) These non-verbal, though conversational,
activities to which the word paralanguage refers are far too diverse, too
little codified, too uninvestigated, and too insufficiently understood, to
be given the air of unity which a noun confers on them; so, having used
'paralanguage' for the title of my paper, I shall, as far as I can, from
now on avoid it. The adjective *paralinguistic* (which was the first of all
these terms to be coined) seems to me, however, much more innocu-
ous, with less power to mislead; and I shall therefore prefer to speak of
paralinguistic phenomena, or behaviour, or activities, rather than of
paralanguage.

Paralinguistic phenomena are neither idiosyncratic and personal, on the one hand, nor generally human, on the other. They must, therefore, be culturally determined, and so, as one would expect, they differ from social group to social group. They differ a great deal, and the differences go with language differences, even with dialect differences within languages, though they sometimes cut across linguistic boundaries. These aspects of human behaviour are bound therefore to interest language teachers, psychiatrists, anthropologists, speech therapists, and, of course, linguists and phoneticians too. Their systematic investigation started comparatively recently, though a desultory interest in them is of long standing. However, a great deal has been done during the last few years – particularly, interestingly enough, by, or in collaboration with, psychiatrists; and I would like here to summarise, sometimes critically, what has so far been accomplished in this area.

Paralinguistic phenomena are non-linguistic elements in conversation. They occur alongside spoken language, interact with it, and produce together with it a total system of communication. They are not necessarily continuously simultaneous with spoken words. They may also be interspersed among them, or precede them, or follow them; but they are always integrated into a conversation considered as a complete linguistic interaction. The study of paralinguistic behaviour is part of the study of conversation: the conversational use of spoken language cannot be properly understood unless paralinguistic elements are taken into account.

All animals communicate with each other by means of noises, bodily movements, and postures, and human beings are no exception; they too communicate by acts which are not different in kind. But human beings have language as well, and these more primitive communicative acts have often become entangled with spoken language when used in conversation, and hence become paralinguistic. Of course, plenty of other 'animal-like' communicative acts are used in various circumstances by human beings, but not as part of conversation: they are then not paralinguistic . This is perhaps a good point to try to delimit the application of 'paralinguistic' rather more strictly than some writers have done. Paralinguistic activities must (*i*) communicate, and (*ii*) be part of a conversational interaction. These two requirements rule out several sorts of activity which have at times been put together with paralinguistic activities. They rule out, for example, a nervous twitch of the eyelid which some people have while talking, since it does not communicate, and many personal mannerisms and tics, since they do not either; and they rule out, for example, the act of taking one's hat off, or a 'wolf whistle', which communicate but do not enter into conversation. (They may initiate one.) Moreover, to be accounted paralinguistic an element in conversation must, at least potentially, be consciously controllable: hoarseness may communicate the fact that one has a cold, but it is not a paralinguistic element in conversation.

We see then that paralinguistic behaviour is non-verbal communication, but not all non-verbal communication is paralinguistic. I have just limited the application of the word, compared to the way it is used by some other writers; I should now like to widen its current application in an important respect. This is connected with a second reason why I do not like the noun *paralanguage* being used in this field. It inevitably runs the risk of being brought into association with that rather special meaning given to the word *language* by certain linguists today who, following Bloomfield, say it can only be 'the noise you make with your face'. If language is this, then – it will be said – paralanguage too must be facial noises. And, in fact, this is the way the word paralanguage is used by most people nowadays. When systematic investigation of the field first started, in America, the word *metalinguistic* was (not very happily) chosen for these non-linguistic elements in conversation (Smith, 1950), and they were divided into two classes, called *kinesics* and *vocalisations* (another rather unhappy term) – roughly, elements due to movements and elements due to sounds. When the term *paralanguage* was introduced (see Trager, 1958, for the early history of these studies) it was applied only to what earlier had been called vocalisations, and kinesics pursued a largely independent existence. This has been a pity. Parallels between the two have been obscured, and kinesics has expanded to include the study of all human bodily movement and posture, whether paralinguistic or not.

I would therefore go back to the early days, and apply the word paralinguistic to both movements and sounds. It is convenient for descriptive purposes to have this dichotomy of paralinguistic elements into *visible* movements and postures and *audible* movements and postures (as many have pointed out, there is a strong gestural aspect about sounds produced by the vocal organs), but it should not be taken to imply difference of function between them in conversation. I do not think there is any. (I would suggest it might be an advantage to restrict the word *kinesics* to the study of non-conversational bodily movements of all kinds.)

If we start examining visible paralinguistic elements, we find another dichotomy, a functional one, useful here, which I suggested some years ago (Abercrombie, 1954). This dichotomy is into those elements which *can* be *independent* of the verbal elements of conversation, and those which *must* be *dependent* on them. A participant in a conversation may nod his head, for example, at the same time as he says the word 'yes'; or he may nod but say nothing – the nod will still communicate. This, therefore, is an *independent* paralinguistic element – it *can* occur alone, though it does not have to. Manual gestures of emphasis, on the other hand, must always accompany spoken words, and communicate nothing without them. These therefore are *dependent* paralinguistic elements.

Much of dependent visible paralinguistic behaviour comes under the heading of posture – the general way in which the whole body is disposed, either when sitting or standing during conversation. Posture goes through a series of changes while people converse (Scheflen, 1964): legs are crossed or uncrossed, participants lean forward or back, elbows are placed on tables, and so on. These changes in posture have a punctuative role in conversation: they indicate the beginnings and endings of contributions to the interaction, show when a point has been made, make clear the relations of participants to each other at any given moment. They are not, as might be supposed, random. The number of postures used in any given culture appears to be limited, and their configurations are determined culturally: Englishmen, we are told by Scheflen, cross their legs differently from Americans. (The study of posture already has its own name in some quarters: 'body semantics'.)

Conversations take place most commonly in the world, perhaps, while the participants are standing up. The distance at which they stand from each other is then of paralinguistic importance, and moreover may vary greatly from culture to culture. Each person unconsciously adopts the conversational proximity appropriate to situations in his own culture; the use of the wrong distance – whether too close or too far away – can give offence (Hall, 1964). (The study of the proximity of conversationalists also already has a name: 'proxemics'.)

It is probably necessary to distinguish at least three more dependent ingredients in visible paralinguistic communication, each making its own contribution to the interaction: gesture, facial expression, and eye contacts between the participants. Gesture is superimposed on posture, involves less of the body at any one time, and changes more rapidly. The amount of gesture that accompanies the verbal elements of conversation varies very much between cultures, as has often been pointed out, and so do the gesture-movements themselves. Much of facial expression is probably idiosyncratic and not to be accounted paralinguistic, though some of it undoubtedly is in some cultures. It is characteristic of other cultures that changes in facial expression are absent in conversation ('dead-pan'). The rôle of eye contacts in conversation is only recently beginning to be understood (Argyle, 1967)

Gesture and facial expression supply the independent visible elements in paralinguistic communication: shrugs, nods, winks, and so on. ('Gesture languages' or 'sign languages', whether of the deaf or of American Indians, are, as their name indicates, linguistic and not paralinguistic; they are systems of communication which are structured as language.)

The same dichotomy, into independent and dependent elements, is useful for handling audible elements of paralinguistic behaviour also. Independent elements are what are usually called *interjections,* and examples are easy to find in all languages. They are characterised by the fact that they do not follow the normal phonological rules of the language. In English we have recognised ways of spelling many of them – tut tut, whew, uh-huh, ahem, humph, sh, ugh – though one could not pronounce them from the spelling unless one already knew what the interjection was.

Dependent audible elements, which are extremely varied, might all be put together under another popular term, *tones of voice.* They are produced by variations from the social *linguistic* norm in features of voice dynamics (Abercrombie, 1967, p. 95) – loudness, tempo, register, tessitura, and others; and also by 'talking through' sobs, yawning, laughter, and so on. A large number of categories have been developed by some writers (Trager, 1958, Crystal and Quirk, 1964) for dealing with them.

I have simply tried here to indicate briefly the state of our knowledge of paralinguistic phenomena at the present time. Their investigation has perhaps not made the progress it should have done in some directions, and this is for diverse reasons: because of the initial unfortunate separation of the visible and the audible components; because of over-categorisation – too much taxonomy without enough to classify; and because linguists have left too much of the work to others. There is an urgent need for the comparative study, over as much of the world as possible, of the full range of paralinguistic phenomena – the kind of thing for which the linguistic fieldworker is best fitted.

Fact-finding, not theorising, is what is wanted at this present juncture. True, fact-finding needs a theoretical framework within which to be conducted, but at this stage categories should be kept flexible, not allowed to proliferate, and regarded mainly as heuristic rather than explanatory. The difficulties – and the expense – of investigation should not, of course, be underrated. Talking films seem essential for obtaining data, and they would probably have to be clandestinely taken, 'candid camera' fashion, to be of real value, which raises difficult moral problems about invasion of privacy. There is also the problem of devising a notation adequate for a paralinguistic text parallel with the linguistic one. The most ambitious attempt at this so far is probably Pittenger, Hockett, and Danehy (1960); other examples of notations and texts can be found in Birdwhistell (1954), Crystal and Quirk (1964), Austin (1965) and others. Sybille Bedford (1958) accompanied her account of the trial of Dr Adams by well-observed notes on the paralinguistic behaviour of the participants, though they are hardly adequate for scientific analysis. A good example of reporting on paralinguistic facts from a linguistic fieldworker is Revill (1966), – though here one meets a new danger in this field, the use of the 'amateur actor'. The investigator asks a subject to demonstrate how he would show distaste, or anger, or fear, and so on; but most people unfortunately, are bad amateur actors, and information so obtained must often be unreliable.

At this point it is appropriate to ask what sort of things are all these paralinguistic elements communicating in a conversational exchange? The answer sometimes given is that they are communicating attitudes and emotions, the linguistic side of the interchange being more 'referential'. But this is not really satisfactory. Paralinguistic elements are often clearly 'referential' – many independent gestures, for instance, which can even be translated directly into words such as 'tomorrow', or 'money'. And on the other hand linguistic elements in a conversation may often communicate attitudes or emotions.

It seems to me a possible hypothesis, in the present state of our knowledge, that in all cultures conversation communicates more or less the same total of 'meaning' of all kinds – sense, feeling, tone, intention; or however one wants to divide up referential and emotive components. Where cultural groups differ, however, is in the way the total information is distributed over the linguistic and the paralinguistic elements of the conversation. For instance, Jules Henry (1936) reports that among the Kaingang of Brazil concepts of degree and intensity are communicated by such things as changes in pitch, facial expression, and bodily posture, though we communicate these things by formal linguistic devices. On the other hand, in Dakota, an American Indian language, an emotional state such as annoyance, which with us would be communicated in conversation by facial expression or tone of voice, has formal linguistic expression by means of a particle added at the end of the sentence (of normal phonological structure, and therefore not an interjection).

Almost anything can be communicated linguistically, and almost anything paralinguistically. What is to be regarded as linguistic and what as paralinguistic depends not on the nature of what is communicated, but on how it is communicated – whether by formal systems and structures, in which case it is linguistic; or not, in which case it is paralinguistic.

REFERENCES

D. Abercrombie, 'Gesture', *English Language Teaching, 9, 3, 1954* (Reprinted in *Problems and Principles in Language Study*, London: Longmans 1956.)

D. Abercrombie, *Elements of General Phonetics,* Edinburgh: Edinburgh University Press, 1967.

M. Argyle, *The Psychology of Interpersonal Behaviour,* Harmondsworth: Penguin, 1967.

M. W. Austin, 'Some social aspects of paralanguage', *Can. J. Linguistics*, 11, 1965, p. 31.

S. Bedford, *The Best We Can Do,* Harmondsworth: Penguin, 1958.

R. L. Birdwhistell, *Introduction to Kinesics,* University of Louisville, 1954.

J. B. Carroll, 'The analysis of verbal behaviour', *Psychol. Rev.*, 51, 1944, p. 102.

H.C. Conklin, 'Linguistic play in its cultural context', *Language,* 35, 1959, p. 631.

M. Critchley *The Language of Gesture,* London: Edward Arnold, 1939.

D. Crystal, and R. Quirk, *Systems of Prosodic and Paralinguistic Features in English*, The Hague: Mouton, 1964.

L. W. Doob, *Communication in Africa,* New Haven and London: Yale University Press, 1961.

D. Efron, *Gesture and Environment*, New York: King's Crown Press, 1941.

E. T. Hall, *The Silent Language,* New York: Doubleday, 1959 (Also Premier Book Paperback, 1961).

E. T. Hall, 'Silent assumptions in social communication', ch. iv in *Disorders of Communication* (ed. D. M. Rioch and E. A. Weinstein), Baltimore, 1964.

F. Hayes, 'Gestures: a working bibliography', *Sth. Folklore q.,* 21, 1957, p. 218.

J. Henry, 'The linguistic expression of emotion,' *Am. Anthrop.* 38, 1936, p. 250.

M. Key, 'Gestures and responses: a preliminary study among some Indian tribes of Bolivia', *Stud. Linguistics,* 16, 1962, p. 92.

W. Lamb, *Posture and Gesture: An Introduction to the Study of Physical Behaviour,* London: Duckworth 1965.

H. Levin, H. and I. Silverman, 'Hesitation phenomena in children's speech', *Language and Speech,* 8, 1965, p. 67.

H. Maclay and C. E. Osgood, 'Hesitation phenomena in spontaneous English speech',*Word,* 15, 1959, p. 19.

R. E. Pittenger and H. L. Smith 'A basis for some contributions of linguistics to psychiatry'*Journal for the Study of Interpersonal Processes,* 20,1957, p.61.

R. Pittenger, C. F. Hockett and J.J. Danehy, *The First Five Minutes,* Ithaca, NY: Paul Martineau, 1960.

P. M. Revill, 'Preliminary report on para-linguistics in Mbembe', Appendix viii in K. L. Pike, *Tagmemic and Matrix Linguistics Applied to Selected African Languages,* Ann Arbor: University of Michigan Center for Research on Language and Language Behaviour, 1966.

E. Sapir, *Abnormal Types of Speech in Nootka,* Ottawa: Department of Mines Geological Survey, 1915.

A. E. Scheflen, 'The significance of posture in communication systems', *Psychiatry: Journal for the Study of Interpersonal Processes,* 27, 1964, p. 316.

H. L. Smith, *The Communication Situation,* Washington: Foreign Service Institute (mimeographed), 1950.

G. L. Trager, 'Paralanguage: a first approximation', *Stud.Linguistics,* 13, 1958, p. 1.

W. E. Welmers, 'Non-segmental elements in foreign language learning', *Monograph Ser. Languages and Linguistics,* 7, 1954, p. 130.

C. Wolff, *A Psychology of Gesture,* London: Methuen, 1945.

14

Encounter with Aphasia

Lecture to postgraduate students in Applied Linguistics, Edinburgh.

Most people are familiar with the word *aphasia*, a general term for disturbance of language functions which results from damage to the brain caused by such things as a tumour, a stroke, a fractured skull, a bullet through the head. The damage may have permanent linguistic consequences, or temporary ones only. A clot of blood, for example, may impair brain functions for a time, but may eventually dissolve, leaving things as they were before it formed.

Strictly speaking, if one goes by its etymology, *aphasia* ought to mean the complete loss of all linguistic ability – it comes from the Greek word meaning 'speechlessness', with the privative or negative prefix *a-* in front. It has always been used for partial loss of linguistic ability as well, however, though some purists have objected, claiming that *dys*phasia would be a more appropriate term in such cases. I shall use aphasia in the general sense, and the word aphasic for the person who suffers from it. Many other terms can specify the nature of the damage more exactly: alexia, dyslexia, agraphia, dyslalia, dysphemia, acalculia.

I have no professional qualifications for talking about the subject: I am strictly an amateur. The people professionally concerned with aphasia are neurologists, neurosurgeons, psychologists, anatomists, physiologists, speech therapists – all people with strong medical affiliations. However, aphasia is an affliction whose symptoms are linguistic, and I feel any student of linguistics has the right to take an interest in the field, even if only amateurish. As a matter of fact, when I was a postgraduate student of linguistics, more particularly phonetics, at University College London, the recommended general reading list included various works on aphasia. (I do not know if this is still the case.) I found them fascinating, but in spite of the topic's linguistic interest, linguists have not written very much on the subject; though there is Roman Jakobson's well-known *Child Language, Aphasia, and Phonological Universals*, which appeared in English translation, published by Mouton, in 1968.

My interest in the subject came originally from reading the books and articles recommended to me as a student; but two quite unconnected things happened later which greatly enlarged my understanding of what I had already read, and which provide some justification for my talking about the subject.

The first of these arose out of the fact that I was in Egypt during the war. I happened to run across, in Cairo, a neurologist whom I used to know quite well in London. He was now in the army and working in the newly formed neurological unit at the Fifteenth Scottish Hospital, a big military hospital in Cairo. The unit was concerned with headwounds which resulted in aphasia; I think I am right in saying that anyone in the Middle East with a headwound which affected his language ability finished up in that hospital. It was quite near where I lived, incidentally. This neurologist, knowing of my interest in linguistic problems, invited me to meet some of his patients, and to talk to his colleagues in the unit. I did so, and subsequently paid many visits to the hospital. Hence I saw a large number of aphasics, talked to them a lot, and got to know some of them quite well. So I had living illustrations of the various kinds of case histories which before I had only read about. And I was able to talk to doctors and surgeons with wide experience of aphasia. Headwounds, I should point out, were very common at that time, often accompanied by no other injuries. Many resulted from putting one's head out of a tank at an inappropriate moment.

That was the first thing which perhaps gives me the right, even if only an amateur, to talk about aphasia. The second thing was that I got married, also in Cairo. I married an aphasic wife. I know husbands and wives often believe that their spouses are aphasic; but mine had suffered genuine aphasia, though she had completely recovered before I married her. She was able to give me a fascinating and detailed account of what the experience had been like. She had become aphasic when, sitting on a beach with some friends, a very large and powerful man chasing a football thrown in the air failed to notice her, and his knee crashed against her left temple. As a result her skull was fractured, and although she did not lose consciousness she almost immediately became completely aphasic: unable to understand, or say, a word.

Visiting and talking to the headwound cases at the Fifteenth Scottish Hospital was not the harrowing experience that one might expect. Certainly, I saw sights that were upsetting to a squeamish person like me; but many of the patients hardly seemed ill at all. They did not have their heads swathed in bandages, but only a small piece of sticking plaster over the small bullet hole. They were astonishingly cheerful (about which I will say more later). Often they were not in bed but dressed and up and about, and sometimes it was difficult to tell there was anything wrong with them at all. They could often converse at length without making any mistakes. There were sometimes dramatic surprises. I once went into a ward where there was a young officer in uniform, walking around, whom I took to be a visitor like myself. We talked for a while; and then a doctor came up, greeted us both, then to my surprise said to the officer, 'Please touch your left ear with your right index finger.' This he was quite unable to do; he felt all over his left hand, but confessed he could not find his ear there; and I realised I had been talking to a patient. (This kind of inability is called 'agnosia'; it seems always to be accompanied by aphasia of various kinds.) I will refer to this officer again; he turned out to be a most interesting case.

In the early days of research into aphasia, the main theoretical problem, on which there were divided opinions, was whether different language faculties were localised in different parts of the brain, so that damage to one part would produce a different disturbance from damage to another part; or whether there was no localisation. By the time of the beginning of the Second World War it seemed to be generally agreed that the localisation theory was the correct one. I have heard that this is not so strongly believed now as it was then. There is no doubt, however, that, if you are right-handed, aphasias are caused by damage to the left temporal lobe of the brain. But it seems to be doubtful whether specific disorders can be more exactly localised. However, the members of the neurosurgical unit in Cairo believed, or at least hoped, that the exact point of damage to the brain could be deduced from the nature of the language disorder which the patient exhibited.

This may have been an exceptionally propitious period for the study of localisation, because opportunities for examining casualties of the sort dealt with at the Fifteenth Scottish Hospital are normally rare. The bullet wounds often resulted in damage being confined to a small area of the brain, the bullet often staying inside the head. Before 1940 such a wound would probably have been fatal: the patient would have died of meningitis. There would have been no chance of studying any language disorders the wound may have caused. The antibiotics had just come in, however; the sulfa drugs (penicillin was not yet in use) saved the lives of many of the most interesting and valuable aphasics (which sounds a callous way of putting it). And not very long after the war modern high-velocity rifles came into use which delivered bullets at a speed that made a terrible mess of the brain, instead of a neat puncture. Perhaps only during that short period were patients available whose symptoms would clearly support the localisation hypothesis.

Types of aphasia have traditionally been classified on an anatomical basis, a physiological basis, or a psychological basis; or on a mixture of any of these. Many neurologists have expressed dissatisfaction with this; but a purely linguistic classification has not, as far as I know, been put forward, though Jakobson suggested one should be. I suggest such a classification might be possible, starting with a distinction between disorders involving the medium, on the one hand, and the language carried by the medium, on the other; in the former case distinguishing the aural from the visual medium, and in the latter case distinguishing the lexicon from the grammar; and in all cases distinguishing expressive, or motor, from receptive, or sensory, disorders. (In parenthesis, it is necessary here to distinguish, from the disorders we are concerned with, kinds of brain damage which impair our control over the *physical production* of the medium. Paralysis, to varying degrees, of the organs used in talking – lips, or tongue, for example – or paralysis of the arm, will gravely affect ability to use the spoken or written medium. But that is not the kind of disability that comes under aphasia, which manifests itself when control of the various organs concerned is unimpaired.)

It is necessary to distinguish between the aural and the visual medium, one of which may be impaired in its use while the other is not. One very remarkable patient I met could write, but was quite unable to read. I found it incredible when told of him until I saw the patient writing a letter home. He wrote the letter pretty well (though not perfectly), but he had to have another patient standing behind him to tell him where he had got to whenever he paused: although he had just written something, he was quite incapable of reading it back.

The brain damage this patient had received, therefore, affected the visual medium in its receptive aspect only – and not very much else. He could manage the aural medium in both receptive and expressive aspects, and could manage the language, as distinct from medium, fairly well. I say 'fairly well' because it seemed to be the case that impairment of any aspect of linguistic ability entailed some falling off – maybe not a lot – of all other aspects. And the sole inability to use the written medium receptively was rather exceptional: most patients had more than one thing wrong with them.

This patient was a complete alexic. I also had to do with a rather interesting partial one, a *dys*lexic. This was the young officer I have already mentioned who could not find his left ear. He was a particularly interesting case because of his considerable knowledge of languages. To start with, he was a classical scholar, and therefore knew Greek and Latin. He also knew French, German, Italian, Hebrew, Arabic, and modern Greek. His knowledge of all those was almost completely lost, but he could read his mother tongue, English, to a certain extent. He was unable to write English. I noticed, when he was asked to read aloud, that common grammatical words caused him the most trouble, and one of the worst was *the*, the definite article. He almost invariably stopped when he came to it, saying 'I know that word perfectly well; what *is* it?' It is disconcerting when someone with whom you have just been having a serious conversation about post-war town planning has a difficulty like this. But the strange thing was the manner in which he could be made to recognise the word; it was one of the doctors who demonstrated this. If the patient took a pencil and copied the word at which he was stuck directly below it, he immediately knew what the word was, and said 'the', or whatever it was. He would nevertheless still be mystified next time he came to it.

I got to know this patient quite well, and oddly enough I met him by chance in the street in London after the war. He had made a complete recovery, and it is interesting that all his languages had come back to him – though not at once, but successively in the order in which he had learnt them.

This same patient, incidentally, had difficulty with numbers, or at least behaved towards them in an odd way. When asked his age, he replied very rapidly 'ten, twenty, one, two, three, four, twenty-four', which was correct. He took a very long time over fairly simple mental arithmetic, but always got the answer right, so he could not be called an acalculic.

Others who had difficulty with numbers were far worse, and were genuine acalculics. A young officer from Scotland, when asked his age, said 'four', but added thoughtfully 'I must be older than that.' He changed it to 'forty' then to '24', which were both wrong. He was able, incidentally, to *write* his age correctly; it was 30.

It seems that reading and writing, if one can be impaired but not the others, must have different centres in the brain, though we are accustomed to thinking of them as inseparable. In this connection it is interesting to recall that in seventeenth- and eighteenth-century schools in England 'the two arts were very sharply divided', as J. W. Adamson has put it (*The Illiterate Anglo-Saxon*, Cambridge, 1946, p. 38); writing being treated in schools so much later than reading that most people never reached it.

One of the commonest types of aphasia is called *nominal* aphasia. It concerns vocabulary, that is to say not the *medium* but the *language*, and typically it is nouns that are affected, hence the name. The noun cannot be produced when it is wanted, though the patient may use the noun easily enough when attention is not focussed on it. (Everybody suffers from this to some extent, particularly with proper names – 'proper nominal aphasia', it could be called.)

Nominal aphasia is one of the first things for which the doctors test a patient. The patient is shown an object – a pen, a key, a handkerchief, or other common everyday object – and asked 'what's that?' Sometimes a nominal aphasic is unable to give an answer; sometimes the answer is quite wrong; sometimes a description is given – 'what you write with' – showing the patient has had no problem in recognising the object. At other times the patient might get it right; but I found it curious (though the doctors had not noticed up to then) that patients often – some of them always – put the definite article in front, and said 'That's the pen', not 'That's a pen'. Maybe they were simply alluding to the fact that they had been through all this before. Or maybe there was a deeper reason. There is a theory that even when the name seems correct, the word is not being used in the normal way: it is called 'pseudo-naming' (see an interesting article 'Naming and pseudo-naming' by Kurt Goldstein, in the periodical *Word*, 2, 1946). Normally when naming something we are assigning it to a class. Pseudo-naming is treating the word like a proper name, an individual name . Which is why perhaps it is so easily lost. Being asked to name a common object is not, of course, a common situation in real life, though Henry Reed's poem 'Naming of Parts' illustrates how at times it may occur.

I came across no case of a *phoneme* being lost from a person's speech, though Jakobson reports such cases in his book mentioned earlier. He also reports cases of the distinction between two phonemes being lost, which I also never found. But mispronunciations of various kinds occurred commonly enough. One patient, for example, called a spoon a 'speen'. (He was dissatisfied with this, but was unable to get it right.) The same patient called a banana a 'banayna'. This sent him into fits of laughter as soon as he had said it; but he was unable to explain why it seemed funny, or what was wrong with it. Another patient, wishing to talk about the field cashier called him the 'fieldy cashier'. He said this once or twice, but then changed it to 'field calshier'. He never succeeded in getting it right. Disorders of this kind were not common. The claim that a phoneme is purely a descriptive unit and has no reality has some support if it is true that a phoneme is not lost in the way that a word is lost.

It is curious that in no case did I come across an example of *intonation* being disturbed. I cannot explain this; perhaps I failed to notice it. However, one gathers from the literature on aphasia that the features most resistant to disturbance by brain damage are rhythm and intonation. Even when all articulation is absent, some aphasics produce utterances in which the syllables, and therefore the rhythm, and also the intonation are preserved; so that what is intended to be 'Are you going?' comes out as 'ah ah ah ah?' I did not have the luck to hear an example of this; it is evidence, however, of the reality of the syllable. I heard a few examples of disintegration of articulation, usually in isolated words; they were usually corrected. For example a patient said a very sloppily articulated 'foosh' on one occasion; this turned out to be 'fruit', which he was later able to say correctly.

A complete, 100 per cent aphasic is someone who has lost the ability to use both spoken language and written language, both receptively and expressively. I met several in the hospital. Naturally there was nothing of linguistic interest to be learnt from them. It is said that sometimes they could communicate by gestures, but I had no evidence of that.

I learnt something of what it is like to be a complete aphasic, however, from my wife's reminiscences. Since, after her accident, there were no external signs of injury, the friends who were with her were very puzzled at her behaviour. She appeared normal, and yet she would not answer their questions; she was suspected of leg-pulling. She has described how odd it seemed to be surrounded by people making strange and incomprehensible noises, but noises that clearly concerned her. It was amusing, rather than alarming. She found it was frustrating though, to be unable to make her wishes clear. She was in shock, felt cold, and wanted a blanket; but was, of course, unable to ask for one. In short, she knew that there was such a thing as language; but she was unable to participate in it.

Her aphasia was due to a blood clot, and only lasted four days (she was of course taken to hospital as soon as it was realised there was something very wrong). The return of her ability to understand language preceded by a little the return of her own ability to talk.

Aphasia, it may be thought, could throw some light on the so-called Whorfian hypothesis. Benjamin Lee Whorf held that it is our language which gives us the categories into which we sort our experiences and thoughts. But the structure and vocabularies of different languages provide different categories, with the result that speakers of different languages do not think about the world and construct theories about it in the same way. (Whorf has been accused of claiming that language differences make people *perceive* things in the world differently; but he was talking, not about the immediate perception, but about the way what is perceived is categorised.) People speaking different languages may segment the world differently, generalise about it differently. We sort our experiences into categories given us by our language.

Someone who becomes a nominal aphasic will lose the sorting categories together with the words on which they depend. An interesting fact may be connected with this. I mentioned earlier that many of the patients in the Scottish Hospital were cheerful – unreasonably cheerful, one might say. The members of the neurosurgical unit used to say that one of the patients' symptoms was euphoria. In the account that my wife gave of her aphasic experience she too mentions that, in spite of the disconcerting nature of what had happened to her, she was very euphoric. She attributed this, afterwards, to the feeling of pleasure she had at being liberated from all the categories she had grown up with: as if every object she perceived was an individual and not a representative of a class. She particularly said that all colours seemed more brilliant. She experienced reality, in other words, more directly. Perhaps the curious euphoria of many of the patients in the Fifteenth Scottish Hospital had the same cause – the feeling of freedom from traditional categories. Certainly many of them had little enough objective reason to feel cheerful.

This account of my encounter with aphasics has been somewhat anecdotal, I fear, but I hope it has shown that the topic can have interest and value for linguists.

Index

Abercrombie, David
- Assistant Anglais, Lycée Louis-le-Grand, Paris, 6
- at Edinburgh University, 10, 48, 54, 70
- at Leeds University, 9–10, 37
- at the London School of Economics, 7, 9
- at the Quinzaine Anglaise held in the Sorbonne, 5
- at University College London, 1–6, 38, 45–6, 109
- his Cardinal Three, 3, 40
- his definition of RP, 48
- his first meeting with Daniel Jones, 37–8
- his interest in writing systems, 5
- his M.A. thesis, 3, 37, 38
- his marriage, 110
- his meeting with Paul Passy, 7
- his work on the history of shorthand, 5
- his work with C. K. Ogden, 8
- his work with Melian Stawell on Cretan scripts, 4–5
- his work with Robert Bridges and Mrs Bridges, 4–5
- in Cairo, 110–5
- on features of voice dynamics, 105
- on gesture, 104
- student at the Institut de Phonétique in Paris, 6, 38
Abercrombie, Lascelles, 37
Abercrombie, Mary, 110, 115–6
acalculia, 109, 113
accent
- a term often used as a synonym of 'stress', 71, 82
- definition of, 83
- existing only at the lexical level, 82
- is ineffable, 83
- possible realisations of, 83
accent(s)
- differences of phonetic realisation between, 55, 57, 67
- distribution differences between, 55, 56–7, 61–2
- structural differences between, 55–6
- systemic differences between, 55, 56, 57–67
accent(s) of English
- choice of, to be represented in reference books, 89
- heard on television and radio, 51
- of Prime Ministers, 51, 57
- rhotic and non-rhotic, 55–6, 59, 89
- see also pronunciation models; Received Pronunciation of English; Scottish Standard English
accent bar, the, in England, 50–1
accented syllable, 82–3, 86
acute syllable, 86
Adamson, J. W., 114
Advisory Committee on Spoken English, BBC, 37, 49
agnosia, 111
agraphia, 109
air-pressure, sub-glottal, 81
air-stream (mechanism), pulmonic, 81–2
Aitken, A. J., 54, 60, 71
Aitken's Vowel, 60–1
Aldridge, William, 95, 100
alexia, 109, 113
Allen, J. P. E., 101